Praise for *Small Habits Create Big Change*

"In *Small Habits Create Big Change*, Rebecca Branstetter moves beyond the cliches of teacher self-care. She makes the connection between striving for equity and teacher self-regulation in her concept of co-thriving that prioritizes adult wellness in the service of supporting students with behavioral, emotional, or learning differences. She shows us that this doesn't happen magically but through small habits that preserve adult joy and thriving."

—**Zaretta Hammond,**
Teacher-Educator and Author of
Culturally Responsive Teaching and the Brain

"This book is filled with clear, practical, and research-based advice to help educators focus on their strengths and thrive in the field. From graduate student to seasoned practitioner, all educators will benefit from Branstetter's helpful insights."

—**Celeste M. Malone, PhD, MS,**
Associate Professor of School Psychology, Howard University;
Past President, National Association of School Psychologists

"Given the numerous stressors that educators are dealing with, *Small Habits Create Big Change* is just in time to facilitate more adaptive responses. Grounded in positive psychology, this book contains a wealth of practices that are easy to implement and that will lead to more productive and less stressful lives."

—**Frank C. Worrell, PhD,**
Director, School Psychology Program,
University of California Berkeley

Small Habits Create Big Change

Small Habits Create Big Change

Strategies to Avoid Burnout and Thrive in Your Education Career

Rebecca Branstetter, Ph.D.

JB JOSSEY-BASS™
A Wiley Brand

Jossey-Bass, a Wiley imprint

Published by John Wiley & Sons, Inc., Hoboken, New Jersey.
Published simultaneously in Canada.

For general information on our other products and services, please contact our Customer Care Department within the United States at (800) 762-2974, outside the United States at (317) 572- 3993. For product technical support, you can find answers to frequently asked questions or reach us via live chat at https://support.wiley.com.

If you believe you've found a mistake in this book, please bring it to our attention by emailing our reader support team at wileysupport@wiley.com with the subject line "Possible Book Errata Submission."

Wiley also publishes its books in a variety of electronic formats. Some content that appears in print may not be available in electronic formats. For more information about Wiley products, visit our website at www.wiley.com.

Library of Congress Cataloging-in-Publication Data

Names: Branstetter, Rebecca, author.
Title: Small habits create big change : strategies to avoid burnout and
  thrive in your education career / Rebecca Branstetter.
Description: Hoboken, New Jersey : Wiley, [2025] | Includes index.
Identifiers: LCCN 2024018006 (print) | LCCN 2024018007 (ebook) | ISBN
  9781394238927 (paperback) | ISBN 9781394238934 (adobe pdf) | ISBN
  9781394238941 (epub)
Subjects: LCSH: Teachers—Mental health. | Burn out
  (Psychology)—Prevention.
Classification: LCC LB2840 .B736 2025 (print) | LCC LB2840 (ebook) | DDC
  371.1001/9—dc23/eng/20240521
LC record available at https://lccn.loc.gov/2024018006
LC ebook record available at https://lccn.loc.gov/2024018007

Cover Art & Design: Paul McCarthy

SKY10081510_080924

Contents

Visit https://thrivingstudents.com/smallhabits to access the downloadables in this book.

About the Author

Rebecca Branstetter, Ph.D., is a school psychologist, international speaker, and author on a mission to help children thrive by supporting school psychologists, educators, and families with burnout prevention and practical tools for helping complex learners. She is the founder of Thriving Students Collective® and Thrive Hive TV® Network, online platforms dedicated to equipping K-12 schools with tools to meet the mental health and learning needs of neurodiverse students.

A sought-after speaker and national media expert, Rebecca's expertise has appeared in various publications, including *Huffington Post*, *Washington Post*, NPR, CNN, and *Parents Magazine*. She and her husband are proud parents to two daughters (and two fluffy husky dogs) in the San Francisco Bay Area.

Rebecca also has a TikTok account all about burnout prevention that her middle school daughter has endorsed as "Cringe, but good dancing." Visit https://rebeccabranstetter.com to learn more about Rebecca's work.

Acknowledgments

This book would not be possible without the village of support around me!

My husband, Steven, is my number one supporter, a true marigold. Thank you for always having my back and encouraging me to keep going with my mission every day. And thanks for the amazing headshot, photos, and creative photography genius behind the Thriving Students Collective®!

My daughters never cease to be a source of meaning and inspiration for the work of supporting educators and students. I always thought being a school psychologist would make me a better mom, but the reverse is true – being a mom to my amazing daughters has made me a better school psychologist! Thank you, girls, for letting mommy go to the café for the many hours it took to write this book!

Angela Watson, you are my ride-or-die marigold! Has it really been more than 15 years since we met in the brand new world of the blog-o-sphere? We were writing about burnout prevention in our parallel universes – me on the west coast, writing about supporting school psychologists and you on the east coast, writing about supporting teachers. Our friendship turned into an incredible partnership as we brought our collective passion together, in our *How to Reverse Educator Burnout* course.

This book, an extension of that project, would not have been born without you, my co-passenger in thriving!

Shout out to Byron McClure and Kelsie Reed for their amazing collaboration and input on creating the Thrive-o-gram! Your strengths-based work is changing the world, and I'm honored to be a part of it with you.

I have so many "silent mentors" to thank! When embarking on this project, a number of authors and awesome humans influenced and ignited my passion for writing about this topic, including Shawn Achor, Arianna Huffington, Nataly Kogan, Zaretta Hammond, Julie Levin, James Clear, Tamara Levitt, Nedra Glover Tawwab, and so many more. I can only hope this book will impact others the way your work has impacted mine.

Foreword

Think back to a time in the classroom when you were in a bad mood.

How did you speak to your students?

What kinds of activities did you facilitate?

How much did you accomplish that day?

Compare that to a time in which you had a positive mental affect. You were probably much more patient and understanding with students' shortcomings, willing to engage in more energy-intensive activities and go the extra mile to help students, and were far more productive in your workday.

For this reason, feeling more happiness and positive emotions benefits everyone around you – especially your students, whose daily classroom experience is largely shaped by the moods you exhibit.

And yet so much focus in schools and professional development is centered only on the needs of students. Certainly, we want to devote our energy to the practices that get positive results for kids, but this laser focus on student outcomes can lead to the dehumanization of the adults who teach them.

It creates a cycle in which educators are treated like disposable resources. Their own needs are sidelined, and they're expected to do "whatever it takes" for the good of the kids.

We hear a lot about the "whole child," and schools are under tremendous strain to meet not just the academic needs of kids, but also to attend to their mental health, physical health, dietary and nutrition needs, transportation, housing, clothing, and more.

The thing is . . . teachers have all of these same needs, and if these needs are left unaddressed and unsupported, adults experience negative outcomes, too.

It's not enough for our students to thrive if that's accomplished by burning out the adults in the building and working them to a state of exhaustion.

What if the goal was for teachers to co-thrive WITH students?

What if we looked for the overlap between what's best for kids and what's best for teachers, and found practices that support everyone involved?

That's exactly why Rebecca and I co-created our course called *Reversing Educator Burnout*, and it's why this book now exists. Both are full of specific practices backed by neuroscience that teachers can use to make their classrooms a place where they can co-thrive with students.

Rebecca and I have been friends for well over a decade, and our collaboration on the course was a natural fit. As a school psychologist, she talks about the research and neuroscience of reversing burnout. Then, I chime in with the practical classroom application. Each module of the course also has a guest expert who shares their unique perspective on reversing burnout.

The thing I love most about Rebecca is the way she incorporates humor, playfulness, and fun into everything she does. So, *of course* there's a 60s hippie road trip theme, because why not do regular professional development when you can do it wearing bell-bottoms?

And it's not just a random road trip, either. We're directing you toward a proven path to reversing educator burnout that will lead you to Thrive Town . . . and we're putting you in the driver's seat.

A few caveats:

In this book (and in our course), you will NOT be taking a detour to Toxic Positivity City. This is where we're gaslighting ourselves into believing everything happening in our schools is fine, and we just need to change our mindset in order to feel better.

Let's be clear up front: your mindset is ONE tool for making stressful circumstances easier to handle. We think it's an incredibly powerful tool. But we never want to imply that you should just think happy thoughts all the time and ignore the problems. We want you to feel and embrace the full spectrum of human emotions, and let anger, disappointment, fear, and other uncomfortable emotions push you to create positive change.

You will also NOT be detouring into the dead-end of "self-care as replacement for community care." Self-care can only take you so far, and it's not enough to counteract everything, and it's unfair for the burden to be placed on you to undo all of the mess from your school day all by yourself alone in the evenings.

The stress you're feeling is part of a systemic problem, so therefore it needs systemic solutions. You are not on your own, and this book will provide tools to help you bring passengers on board your journey to Thrive Town. We want you to have allies supporting you in the important work you're doing.

And finally, you're NOT going to detour into One-Size-Fits-All Valley. There are so many factors that impact your experience in education. The way you're treated, the amount of respect you are automatically afforded, the types of demands that are asked of you, and so on are not equal for everyone.

We know that identities of gender, race, ethnicity, and sexual orientation all have an impact on the type of stressors that show up in the job and impact the types of solutions that will be effective. We also know that your years of experience, credentials, ties to the community, and other changeable factors impact the way you experience stressors, and this book will speak to that as well.

Mindset and countering burnout are in many ways very personal journeys – no two educators will take the exact same path. There are many, many ways to get there and we'll share lots of different routes so you can choose the one that is best for you.

Our destination of Thrive Town is a really big place, and when you arrive, you'll find the neighborhood there that you feel comfortable in, with habits and routines and mindset shifts that feel like home to you.

I hope by the end of this journey you'll be convinced that wanting to feel good and be happy is far from a selfish pursuit. An emotionally regulated teacher is going to be more effective. When you're in a higher emotional state, you treat the people around you better and are more responsive to their needs.

Your ability to thrive and feel supported *matters*. When educators thrive, students are in a far more powerful position to co-thrive alongside them.

—Angela Watson

Small Habits Create Big Change

Introduction:
Why I Wrote *Small Habits*

I was huddled under my desk at the school district office, clutching my pregnant belly and hiding from a gunman on campus when I knew.

I knew that I loved my students.

I knew that I was passionate about being a school psychologist.

I knew I was making a difference in the lives of children.

I knew that a self-care bubble bath after work was *not* going to work to keep me from burning out.

I knew that the likelihood of the stressors of being a school psychologist weren't going to change any time soon.

When it was all over, and everyone was safe, I drove home, crying.

I knew that I didn't want to quit, but it felt like quitting was the only solution.

Deep down, I also knew that *something* had to change so I could thrive in the career of my dreams.

But what? How? Was it even possible?

Chances are, if you've picked up this book, you might be wondering the same thing – *how can I sustain my passion for my career in education in such challenging circumstances?* While not everyone has had a dramatic life-threatening moment like the one I described, you have probably had a similar moment of your own, driving home in your car after a hard day, wondering if it's all worth it and how you can rekindle the joy.

That's what this book is about.

But first, here's what this book is *not* about: It's not about you not self-caring enough. It's not about blaming you, the students, families, society, or "the system." It's also not about toxic positivity and pretending it's not stressful to be an educator. And it's definitely not about sacrificing your well-being and nervous system for your "bigger why."

It's about using the neuroscience of wellness and burnout prevention to change what you can and learning how to cope with the rest. It's about your own growth and empowerment. Above all, it's about inspiring hope and giving you practical tools so you can thrive in the career of your dreams.

How the Book Is Organized

Sometimes things come into your life right when you need them. Ironically, the week after the lockdown incident, a publisher reached out to me and asked me to write a book, called *The School Psychologist's Survival Guide*. Ha! The irony! Here I was, on the brink of quitting, and here someone thought I could write a book on how to thrive? The universe is funny like that.

I saw this as a sign that my work in education was not done. I took the deal and started my me-search (excuse me, RE-search) project on how to prevent burnout and thrive in education. I dug into the literature. I interviewed veteran teachers and school psychologists about what kept them going. And do you know what I learned?

It's all about the small things.

Research vs. Reality

For many educators, the research-to-reality gap in schools feels like the Grand Canyon. Standing on one side, we are entrenched in the daily struggle. On the other side, we see what works for kids, what keeps us mentally healthy, and what best practices are. Even if we don't know exactly or have a study citation to prove it, we have a felt sense when things are going well and when things are going off the rails. But we're not sure how to show up on Monday and change the status quo.

We can't even imagine the bridge over the gap and the feat it would take to get there. So, we stay on the side of least resistance, wishing we were on the other side. Or we hope someone will come along with more funding and staff and build us the bridge. And we wait. Y'all I've been waiting for 20 years for reasonable caseloads as a school psychologist. And yet, I always have more students to support than any human could be expected to support in the fictional 40-hour work week of an educator. Isn't there anything we can do NOW?

We can. The neuroscience of wellness and the science of learning is the invisible bridge we need to trust is there to take us to best practices for kids and for ourselves.

When you see that first invisible step become apparent, that's when forward progress begins.

And when you have science to back up your felt sense of best practices, the ideas and practices gain traction and credibility. That's why this book is intentionally grounded in 10 science-backed principles that have been shown to boost your wellness and prevent burnout.

Even more exciting is the link between your wellness and your students' wellness and achievement, a concept I call "co-thriving."

So often, educational wellness initiatives operate in silos. We have staff wellness initiatives over here, with a teacher luncheon, staff shout outs in newsletters, or an appreciation week. Then we have student wellness initiatives over there, with mental health services, special education programs, school-wide social-emotional learning (SEL) programs, positive behavior intervention systems (PBIS), and all the other plethora of acronyms of interventions. Schools frequently organize their interventions in a Multi-Tiered System of Support (MTSS), with Tier 1 supports for all, Tier 2 supports for groups of students who do not respond to Tier 1, and Tier 3 intensive supports for the students with the most need.

The reality is that none of the student interventions at Multi-Tiered Systems of Support (MTSS) are going to work very well without focusing on what I call "Tier 0," which is tending to the educators providing all these supports!

Co-thriving is understanding the reciprocal relationship and virtuous cycle of wellness when we prioritize adult wellness first. While this likely makes sense to you intuitively, because if you're not emotionally well, you have less energy to connect with and support your students, here's some powerful research to back up the assertion:

- **Teacher well-being promotes student well-being and achievement**.
  - When teachers have high psychological functioning and self-awareness, students show a better school experience (e.g. academic performance, engagement, well-being and positive teacher-student interactions).[1]
  - Teacher mental health and well-being is associated with student mental health and well-being and less psychological distress.[2]
  - Teachers' emotions are an important predictor of students' emotions in class. Research shows that teachers' emotions are as important for students' emotions as teachers' instructional behavior.[3]

- **Teacher efficacy enhances teacher well-being and achievement**

  - Teacher efficacy, or the confidence in guiding students toward success and the ability to teach all students successfully, is a strong predictor of student achievement.[4]
  - Collective teacher efficacy, which is the belief that teachers can positively impact their students' learning when they work together, has one of the highest impacts on student achievement.[5]
  - A source of stress for teachers is not feeling efficacious to support students with behavioral, emotional, or learning differences. In a study of general education teachers, only 17% felt that they had the skills to support students with mild disabilities, and yet students with disabilities spend 80% of their day in general education.[6]
  - Existing research suggests that the availability of supports and resources to address students' needs may affect teacher wellness.[7]
  - Unmet student needs may be a potentially critical source of teacher stress. On the flip side, supporting and upskilling educators on helping kids who learn differently has the potential to enhance self-efficacy and reduce stress.[8]

You probably don't need a robust meta-analysis to tell you that it's stressful to go to work every day and not be able to reach and teach your students. Kids acting out, shutting down, or tuning out to the lesson plan you spent all weekend lovingly crafting, can trigger even the most Zen-minded teacher's nervous system. Day in, day out, that takes an emotional toll.

On the other hand, think of the days when you felt joyful, excited, and energetic. Maybe it was a day you finally got through to a student who has been struggling and got to witness an "aha moment." Perhaps you got a new teaching hack or

technology that really worked with your students. How rewarding is that? This drives home the point: When you feel efficacious in your role, it enhances your well-being and your students
benefit as well.

The research simply backs up what we know: When we are
rested, positive, and feel like we have the skills to support our
students' academic, behavioral, and emotional well-being, we
"co-thrive." Our well-being is enhanced, our students' well-
being improves, and students do better academically. There is
something comforting that there's science behind the importance of tending to our well-being, not just as something that
helps us feel better, but is actually essential for our students.
That's why each chapter in this book starts with the "why" behind
the science-backed principle. I'll share the latest research on why
the principle is so important for your career as an educator, and
we will nerd out on the neuroscience that is not only informative
for you, but also for modeling and educating your students on
the same principles to thrive.

Information vs. Transformation

Chances are, many of these principles will be familiar to you, and
will at first glance, seem pretty darn obvious. No one is going to
read Chapter 6 and run to another teacher screaming in excitement, "OMG have you heard about this thing called rest and
downtime?!?"

Information is not transformation!

If it was, we would all be walking around super fit because we
all *know* that we should exercise daily, eat healthy, and get good
sleep. It's about turning that information into practical, doable
habits. Over time, *doing* those habits stack up to new ways of *being*.

The science of micro-habits is one that I've geeked out on
for a long time. Here are seven key principles:

The Myth of Willpower

When we think about changing our behavior, like eating healthy, working out more, or leaving work at work, we fall prey to the myth that changing habits is simply a matter of self-control. This overlooks the complex interplay of environmental cues and emotional triggers that influence behavior. In reality, sustainable habit change often requires restructuring our surroundings and routines to support new behaviors, rather than relying on sheer force of will and inconsistent personal discipline. Just think: is it easier to eat healthy when you have a kitchen stocked with healthy choices or a pantry with tempting sweets? Sure, you can use willpower to resist the sweets, but if the environment is set up for success, you won't have to exhaust your willpower, the choice is made for you.

I love this metaphor for the myth of willpower in changing habits: It's like riding an elephant in an overgrown jungle and believing you, the rider, can forge a new path through using sheer determination to move the elephant, when in fact, it's the well-worn trail – the environment – that often dictates the direction the elephant takes with ease. Creating a new habit is less about the rider's will and more about clearing a new, inviting path for the elephant to follow without resistance.

For example, a well-worn path to wellness could be the routine of starting each morning with a few minutes of mindfulness or deep breathing exercises before students arrive. This practice, over time, becomes a natural and effortless part of your daily routine, providing a stable foundation for a calm and centered presence throughout the day.

Micro-Habits That Are "Too Small to Fail"

There's this nifty trick where you shrink a habit down to something so easy, you can't really mess it up – that's your "too small to fail" habit, and it's a sneaky way to keep you on track without feeling overwhelmed. Just think of the smallest slice of the habit that still feels doable and creates momentum to keep going. Famous habit researcher B.J. Fogg of the Behavior Design Lab at Stanford has popularized this idea by encouraging people to make habits as small as you can, even bordering on ridiculous, because it gives you a small win that makes it easier to move toward your goal.

For example, if you have a bunch of emails to respond to and you don't feel like doing them all, just open your inbox and reply to one, even if it's "I got your email and will get back to you by the end of the week," that's the "too small to fail" habit. Chances are, once you're in there, you'll get momentum to keep going.

I love the metaphor of "eat the frog" for this principle. Mark Twain is often credited with saying, "If the first thing you do each morning is to eat a live frog, you can go through the day with the satisfaction of knowing that that is probably the worst thing that is going to happen to you all day long." Your "frog task" is the most important thing you need to do and tends to be one you procrastinate or put off. Whether it's your inbox or attending your boxing class, we can easily put things off if they feel too big. Just as we break down big tasks into smaller bite-sized chunks for our students, we can do the same thing for ourselves!

I'll also add that the advice to do this task first thing in the morning is wise, because you won't have spent all your willpower yet! It's much easier to build in a small exercise or mindfulness routine in the morning than to muster up the energy after a long day to carve out time for the same tasks when you're physically and emotionally spent.

Making this frog task a small, doable activity that doesn't feel hard can pave the way to success. As James Clear writes in his book, *Atomic Habits*, "Habits are the compound interest of self-improvement" (p.16). What he means is that we are bundles of habits. The little things we do, day in and day out without conscious thought shape who we are. By changing our habits, we make steady progress toward a new way of being that becomes automatic. When we practice a new habit over and over, it becomes second nature, and we don't have to use as much will-power because we are on autopilot. Just think of when you first started to drive a car, how much you had to think about every decision, and you had to have the radio off to focus, and it used up a lot of brain juice. Now, this well-worn habit of driving every day is so on autopilot, you might not even remember driving home from work! This is the goal – shifting our habits so our healthy behaviors become more on autopilot than our unhealthy ones.

The key for creating new habits is to have as little friction for the new habit as possible. There's a ton of friction to go to the gym, for example – the multiple steps of getting dressed, packing work clothes for after the workout, driving there, finding a spot, deciding what to do, how long to do it, showering, changing – is a lot of steps. However, putting on your tennis shoes and walking around the block with your dog, or doing a 10-minute stretching video on YouTube has far less friction, and is a much more doable "frog task" of working out. And if even that feels daunting, you can make it even easier by sleeping in your workout clothes and hav-ing your tennis shoes right by your bed so you can easily and literally roll out of bed and slide into the habit!

Then, when the "I move my body every morning" habit is well established, you can decide if you are ready to ramp it up. Your walk could be a jog, or your 10-minute video can be bumped to a 15-minute one with weights. The key is to "eat the frog" by doing the lowest lift task until it becomes routine.

Keystone Habits

We talked about micro-habits, but let's not forget those big-deal habits, the kind that kickstart a whole bunch of other good habits without you even trying too hard – those are your keystone habits, the real game changers.

For example, sleep, healthy eating, and exercise are keystone habits – when you get a good night's sleep, are fueled by nutritional meals, or keep active, it gives you energy for all the other habits you want to cultivate. Any one of these three keystone habits are valuable, but you might want to start with sleep, which is one of the most powerful interventions for health and well-being.

Sleep   You likely know some of the benefits of good sleep, but let me ask you this: If there were a pill you could take to help with better judgement, more self-control, more creativity, clearing out beta-amyloid (the waste product that builds up in Alzheimer's patients and disrupts cognition), processing your emotions, storing your memories better, and enhanced mood, would you take it? I bet you'd be lined up at the pharmacy for that! That "pill" is sleep, y'all. And despite knowing this intuitively, we can still stay up late scrolling through social media or working late to prepare "just one more thing" for tomorrow, and end up tossing and turning all night with worry about the upcoming day.

You can start with something small, like setting a recurring alarm on your phone for 30 minutes before bedtime to remind you to start your wind-down routine, like putting your smartphone away in another room, out of reach at 9 p.m., and dimming the lights an hour before bedtime; you will start to train your body to facilitate sleep. Oh! And never check your email before bedtime, just in case you get an upsetting email that might disrupt your sleep. (Been there, done that!) In fact, any kind of media (good or bad) before bed can wake up your brain and cost you as much as an hour of sleep on average per night.[9]

Nutrition Start with hydration, which has been shown to improve energy and concentration and reduce fatigue and anxiety. Get one of those snazzy water bottles that is marked with water lines by time of day, so you drink a little at a time all day long.

Healthy snacks and lunch are a natural next step, though for some reason for busy educators, they can go by the wayside when we're stressed or busy. It's a paradox for me that I pack my daughters a perfectly balanced, sugar free lunch every day and then here I go, shoving an old granola bar from the bottom of my work backpack in my face at 2 p.m. because I was too busy to eat lunch! Piggybacking on the habit research, creating environmental conditions for healthy eating so you don't have to use willpower to resist those teacher's lounge donuts, planning out your meals for the week on Sundays, or making extra portions of your healthy dinner to pack for the next day's lunch can set the stage for success.

Exercise One of the sure-fire ways to boost your mood, focus, and sleep quality is exercise. Again, this falls in the "Duh! I already know this information!" category, so the key is to make it a too small to fail habit. Routinize it and build it into your lifestyle one small habit at a time. Sign up for a fun class with a friend, walk around the building during recess to get your blood flowing, do stretches and movement with your students, take the long route to the copier – everything counts!

Something Old, Something New You know how sometimes it's easier to remember to do something new when you tack it onto something you're already doing? That's habit stacking for you – just hooking up a fresh habit to an old one so it sticks better. This concept, popularized by BJ Fogg as "Tiny Habits Recipes" creates a cue for the new habit. Activities, time of day, and location can also be cues, so long as they are really specific.

For example, if you're like me and you have a well-worn habit of making coffee in the morning, you can pair a gratitude practice while it's brewing. The coffee brewing becomes a cue for gratitude. Another example for pairing habits is when you turn on the shower, do a 30-second plank while the water warms up. At school, it may be when the recess bell rings, you take a deep breath in for four counts and breathe out for eight counts. The recess bell becomes a mindfulness bell!

If you're feeling saucy, you can stack even more habits on the initial habit! If you have successfully paired the trigger of a school bell with a mindful breath, you can stack another thing right on top of that, like taking a sip out of your massive water bottle I suggested you buy earlier. The key is to find something that always happens without thinking, like coffee making, turning on the shower, or a recess bell – something that happens daily without fail.

New habits do take time, but it only takes on average 66 days to create a habit, which means that within a few months, you can be on the path to big changes with small habits![10]

Mindset Matters

Our implicit beliefs often unconsciously guide our behavior. When we change our beliefs, changed behavior follows. Here's a sort-of rhetorical question to illustrate this concept: Do you like to be right? Is there any other more satisfying sentence to tell ourselves than, "I was RIGHT!" Probably not! We love to be right, *and so does our brain*. Our brain loves nothing more than to scan for confirmatory evidence of a belief.

For example, when we have an unspoken belief like "I am under-appreciated at work" our brain starts to scan for the opportunity to be right about that. Someone doesn't notice your extra work on a committee? Your brain locks in on that. A parent sends you an obnoxious email about how you're not doing enough? Your brain files that away under "See! I was right!" The problem is, we encode, store, and reinforce this belief with every piece of confirmatory evidence, *even in the face of counter-evidence*. That "thank you" from a principal or an appreciative email from a parent doesn't even register.

The antidote to this negativity bias is to identify a new belief. In the same example, instead of "I am underappreciated" you could say, "I make a difference, whether someone verbalizes their appreciation or not." Then, your brain will start to scan for chances to be right. Suddenly, that smile from a student gets registered as "I made a difference in that student's day." The small "thank you for covering my class while I used the restroom" from a colleague becomes confirmation that you are making a difference, and strengthens the positive mindset that you can give yourself the appreciation you crave from others.

Another example of shifting your mindset to guide behavior is to evaluate what are your beliefs about change. Just as we want our students to have a growth mindset, where they believe that effort pays off, we too need to practice what we preach! When we believe that mistakes are how we learn and grow, we are more patient with our shortcomings. When we truly believe that we can reach that student with a disability, inspire an apathetic student, or change a school culture to embrace wellness, we become more persistent, creative, and take more action to confirm our belief.

Accountability

Accountability starts with clarity. When we write down our goals and intentions for our behavior, we are more likely to do them.

For example, people who genuinely care about voting and intend to vote, can end up not doing it for a variety of reasons. On the flip side, people are more likely to vote when they make a specific plan – when, where, and with whom.[11] The same is true for our wellness goals. Making a vague goal to "work out more" will not be as effective as writing out a plan for working out three times a week with a YouTube video with a favorite yoga instructor from 6:30-7 a.m. on Mondays, Wednesdays, and Fridays.

We can further improve our accountability by partnering up with others (ever notice it's easier to go to the gym to do a new class with a friend?). When we share our goals with a buddy, our success rate increases the chance that we will actually follow through.[12] A recent study found that when participants wrote down their goals and then sent weekly updates on their progress to a friend, they were 50% more likely to be successful than those who kept their goals to themselves.[13]

The benefits of a buddy include:

- Staying motivated and focused on your goals
- Helping you plan and strategize to achieve your goals
- Providing an independent, unbiased perspective to keep you on track
- Reminding you of your goals when you feel discouraged
- Giving you honest feedback and advice for improvement

As you'll learn in Chapter 3, It's important to pick the right kind of accountability buddy! Sharing your goals with someone who will be negative, critical, or someone who just doesn't "get it" can backfire, whereas selectively sharing your goals, with the right people who you believe will provide positive support and accountability can boost your motivation. It's also important to ask your buddy to keep you accountable to the process, not the goal. Are you doing the daily things you said you would do (frog tasks!) is more important than achieving the end goal.

Self-Compassion

Educators tend to have great compassion for our students and others, but then we turn around and beat ourselves up for not getting everything right, or not doing enough. When we make mistakes, we can chastise ourselves for not seeing them coming, and feel terrible. And yet, if a colleague came to us and confessed they made that same mistake and feel like a failure, we'd tell them all kinds of comforting things! The antidote of self-compassion, which you will learn a lot more about in Chapter 8, is essentially treating yourself like you would a best friend or someone you care about deeply.

Research shows that when we treat ourselves with kindness as we learn new habits, instead of criticism, we are more likely to rebound from challenges, persist in our goals, and approach our emotions related to goal-related setback. Dr. Kristin Neff and colleagues have found a number of benefits of self-compassion on goal attainment:[14]

- Self-compassion is positively associated with greater goal progress and well-being in the pursuit of personal goals. Self-compassionate individuals are more able to admit mistakes, modify unproductive behaviors, and take on new challenges.

- Self-compassion is linked to greater intrinsic motivation, a learning orientation, and less avoidance in goal pursuit, which are factors associated with greater goal progress.

- Self-compassion can help individuals cope with the experience of unattainable goals by regulating emotional reactions to setbacks. It can normalize negative feelings and reduce paralyzing perfectionism.

Neff's research has also found that self-compassion is strongly associated with psychological well-being. Higher levels of self-compassion are linked to increased feelings of happiness, optimism, curiosity, and connectedness, as well as decreased anxiety, depression, rumination, and fear of failure. In essence, when we treat ourselves with kindness, we not only persist more on our goals, we also enhance our well-being, which provides further emotional energy for pursuing our goals.

Habits Are a Vote for Who You Are

I've already shared some habit hacks for paving the way for new habits, but there's one more that is essential for success. As James Clear, author of *Atomic Habits*, points out, one of the most overlooked pathways to making change is to start with making it a part of your identity, since "once a person believes in a particular aspect of their identity, they are more likely to act in alignment with that belief" (page 34). He cites research that shows people who say things like "I vote" are less likely to vote than people who say, "I am a voter."[15] He argues that one of the biggest blockers of longstanding change is identity conflict.

Here's an educator example. If you hold the identity of a teacher who is so passionate that you must give 100% to your students every day, and you try to make time for rest and time off, that new habit isn't going to stick because it conflicts with your identity. If you tell yourself that you are a teacher who prioritizes well-being to be emotionally available to your students, then the rest falls right in line with that identity. There are countless educational identity examples:

- I am a workaholic
- I'm not good with self-care
- I am terrible with time management

- I'm not a gym person
- I am bad with work-life boundaries
- I am a perfectionist

Remember how our brains love to be right? These repeated stories we tell ourselves can prevent new habits from taking hold because the behavior is not consistent with our identity. We'll dive into new beliefs throughout this book.

And rest assured, changing your beliefs and behaviors is not about denying reality and being unrealistically positive all the time! It's about orienting your identity toward a new "north star" belief. You may not believe it right away, but all the little behaviors that start to stack up begin to confirm and reinforce the new identity. And since you're an imperfect human, be sure to give yourself grace if you fall back into old habits! If you go off course, you can always chart your way back with your north star.

If that felt like a lot of science dropped on you, not to worry! In each chapter, I embed the research (and how to turn it into reality with micro-habits!) into one of 10 core principles of change.

From What's Wrong to What's Strong

You know that moment when you help a student realize their potential? When they start to believe in themselves? That glorious moment when they start to see themselves as a strong reader, a capable mathematician, or as a leader. It's a magical moment when kids tap into their inner strength and you get to witness them shine, have an "aha moment," or do something for the first time they didn't think was possible.

Now, imagine *you* are the student. You can reach your potential, believe in yourself, and see yourself as a strong and capable educator who can thrive in even the most challenging of circumstances. Imagine how it would feel to go home at the end of the day, knowing you got to use all your skills and talents to make a big impact with students . . . without feeling drained.

That's what the companion assessment to this book, the Thrive-o-gram will help you do. It will help you focus on what's strong, not just what's wrong! Visit www.thrivingstudents.com/thriveogram to take the assessment, and you'll learn:

- Which of the most common "educator burnout traps" you're most likely to fall in . . . and how to avoid them!
- Which of the eight Thrive-o-gram personality types you are . . . and what your core strengths are as an educator.
- How to leverage your strengths to avoid burnout traps and feel uplifted and empowered in your career.

Throughout this book, you'll get practical tips to hit the "happiness reset button" for yourself so you have more joy and work-life balance, all based on your unique Thrive-o-gram profile. So, before you start your journey to thriving, take 10 minutes to discover your top strengths! We will be referencing this assessment throughout the book, to customize strategies for your personality, motivational profile, and strengths. Just like there's no "one size fits all" strategy for our students, there's no one strategy that will work for everyone, so take this assessment and get started!

Take the Assessment

Once you've taken your assessment at www.thrivingstudents.com/thriveogram, you will get your results emailed to you along with a guide for how to interpret the findings. See Figure I.1 for a visual of the types in the Thrive-o-gram and the related strengths for easy reference throughout our journey together!

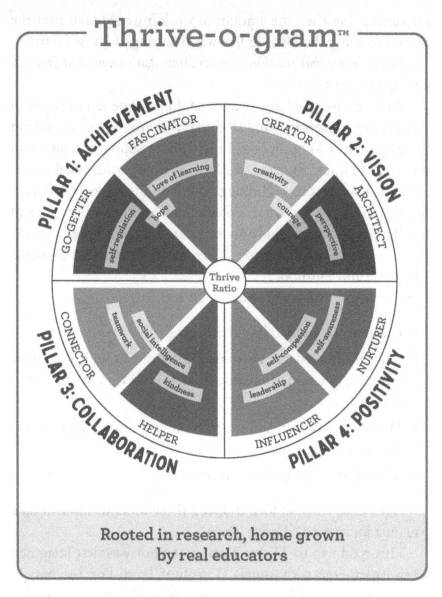

FIGURE I.1 Thrive-o-gram types

Thriving Action Plan

Have you ever sat in a professional development session or a training and wanted to poke your eyes out because it was so boring or irrelevant to what you do all day? Or maybe it was interesting, but then the amount of work it would take after the session to bring the ideas to live was daunting? I know I have!

Isn't it ironic that trainings for educators don't model best practices for how humans learn best?

Well, in case you haven't noticed, I'm a huge fan of research on learning, motivation, and all things thriving, as well as making things practical. When I began my work of supporting adults in schools, I first just thought of all the terrible professional developments I've been in, and thought, "I'll do the opposite of that." But then, I researched what makes adult learning meaningful and fun. These principles guide my organization, Thriving Students Collective (where our motto is, "When we Thrive, Our Students Thrive®") and this book.

Here's what we know about adult learners:

- Content has to be relevant and actionable.[16]
- Upskilling needs to be something you can add *in* to your practice, not something you have to find time to add *on* to your practice.[17]
- Humor helps us retain more content and increases understanding of concepts.[18]
- Metaphor aids learning and retention.[19]

With that, I would love to bring these ideas to life and take you on a journey to "Thrive Town"!

This road trip to Thrive Town metaphor was first imagined when I partnered with Angela Watson of Truth For Teachers in the *How to Reverse Educator Burnout* course. We set out to create this online course for educators that, first and foremost, rejected the notion that your burnout is some sort of personal self-care fail. Or that you need to burn yourself to the ground for your "bigger why" – which is so often the joy of making a difference in the lives of kids.

We looked at unpacking the "upstream" challenges we face, not focusing on "downstream" self-care behaviors to cope with the stress.

This book follows the metaphor of the companion course, *How to Reverse Educator Burnout*, which is available in the Thriving Students Collective® platform for individuals and school districts at www.thrivingstudents.com. If you're the type of person who likes to process information visually or in video form, the companion course is a way to work on these concepts in tandem and go deeper.

If you're a district leader and want to engage your team in a professional learning community, you can take this "roadtrip" with your colleauges! Be sure to check out the facilitator's guide in Appendix B: Journey to Thrive Town: A Guide for School and District Leaders, for ideas on how to lead a team through the book or course together.

Regardless if your learning preference is to read the book alone, have a book club, or pair it with the course, we're going to embark on a road trip of sorts; only *you* get to decide where you want to end up. You get to decide what thriving looks and feels like for you in your career. What is on the other side of the canyon? What are the small micro steps we can take together that feel doable?

We're not going to take any detours to Toxic Positivity Town, stop at the World's Largest Ball of "Your Bigger Why" or swing by the Jeans Emporium where you can erase your stress with a Jeans Day pass!

We're going to take 10 stops along the way to Thrive Town, each a science-backed practice with practical micro-habits and tools on how to apply the research into the reality at your school and in your life.

Just like any road trip, you're going to want to pick up some souvenirs – things that you want to take back home with you to your school. You're going to have souvenirs for yourself, as well as trinkets of information that you can bring back to your students to boost their wellness, too. But like the ginormous black and white sun hat I bought on a beach vacation that looked ah-may-zing in that context but ridiculous in Oakland, only take what works in your context!

Buckle up . . . let's go! (And be sure to check out the Thriving Road Map in the appendix to follow along as you read!)

Discussion Questions:

1. **Resonating Experiences:** The introduction talks about the author's moment of clarity under extreme stress. Share an experience from your teaching career that resonated with you deeply and influenced your approach to education.
2. **Habit Formation in Education:** Reflect on your own experience with forming new habits in your professional life. Which small habits have you successfully integrated into your daily routine that have made a positive impact on your teaching or well-being?
3. **Micro-Habits for Macro Changes:** Discuss the concept of "too small to fail" habits. Have you tried implementing such micro-habits in your practice? If so, what was the outcome, and if not, what is one micro-habit you could start tomorrow?
4. **Challenges of Change:** What challenges have you faced when trying to change behaviors or implement new strategies in your teaching practice? How have you overcome these challenges, or how might you approach them now?
5. **Setting Intentions:** As you begin reading this book, what are your intentions? What do you hope to achieve or learn, and how do you plan to apply this to your educational environment?

Notes

1. L.P. Maricuțoiu, Z. Pap, and E. Ștefancu et al. (2023). Is Teachers' Well-Being Associated with Students' School Experience? A Meta-analysis of Cross-Sectional Evidence. *Educational Psychology Review* 35, 1 (2023). https://doi.org/10.1007/s10648-023-09721-9
2. American Psychiatric Association (2019). Teachers' Mental Health and Well-being Linked to Students' Mental Health and Well-Being. https://www.psychiatry.org/news-room/apa-blogs/teachers-mental-health-well-being-linked-students#:~:text=Researchers%20found%20that%20teachers'%20mental,well%2Dbeing%20of%20their%20students
3. Eva Susan Becker et al. (2014). The Importance of Teachers' Emotions and Instructional Behavior for Their Students' Emotions—An Experience Sampling Analysis. *Teaching and Teacher Education*, vol 43, 15–26. https://www.sciencedirect.com/science/article/abs/pii/S0742051X14000602
4. Ratna Hidayah et al. (2023). The Influence of Teacher Efficacy on Education Quality: A Meta-Analysis. *International Journal of Education Methodology* 9, no. 2, pp. 435–450. https://eric.ed.gov/?id=EJ1391527
5. Visible Learning (2018). Collective Teacher Efficacy (CTE) according to John Hattie. https://visible-learning.org/2018/03/collective-teacher-efficacy-hattie/
6. Stacy Galiatsos et al. (2019). Forward Together: Helping Educators Unlock the Power of Students Who Learn Differently. National Center for Learning Disabilities. https://www.scribd.com/document/411837242/Forward-Together-NCLD-Report
7. Katherine M. Zinsser, Ph.D., et al. (2016). She's supporting them; who's supporting her? Preschool center-level social-emotional supports and teacher well-being. *Journal of School Psychology* 59, pp. 55–66. https://www.sciencedirect.com/science/article/abs/pii/S0022440516300541
8. Alexandra Cox et al. (2018). Teacher Well-Being Is a Critical and Often Overlooked Part of School Health. *Child Trends*. https://www.childtrends.org/publications/teacher-well-being-is-a-critical-and-often-overlooked-part-of-school-health
9. Michael Breus (2024). Technology and Sleep. *Sleep Doctor*. https://sleepdoctor.com/technology/
10. Phillippa Lally et al. (2009). How are habits formed: Modelling habit formation in the real world. *European Journal of Psychology*. https://onlinelibrary.wiley.com/doi/abs/10.1002/ejsp.674
11. David W. Nickerson and Todd Rogers (2010). Do you have a Voting Plan: Implementation Intentions, Voter Turnout and Organic Plan Making. *Psychological Science* vol 21, no. 2 (2010). https://journals.sagepub.com/doi/abs/10.1177/0956797609359326

12. Jeff Haden (2024). Want to Be More Successful? Research Shows an Accountability Buddy Makes a Huge Difference, but With 1 (Literally) Meaningful Catch. Inc. https://www.inc.com/jeff-haden/want-to-be-more-successful-research-shows-an-accountability-buddy-makes-a-huge-difference-but-with-one-literally-meaningful-catch.html

13. Gail Matthews (2007). "The Impact of Commitment, Accountability, and Written Goals on Goal Achievement." *Psychology | Faculty Presentations. 3.* https://scholar.dominican.edu/psychology-faculty-conference-presentations/3

14. Kristin Neff (2024). Publications by Kristin Neff and Colleagues (in Chronological Order). *Self-Compassion.* https://self-compassion.org/the-research/

15. Christopher J. Bryan et al. (2011). Motivating Voter Turnout by Invoking the Self. *Proceedings of the National Academy of Sciences* 108, no. 31. https://www.pnas.org/doi/full/10.1073/pnas.1103343108

16. Michael Wiseman (2022). Adult Learning Theory: 10 Key Principles and Best Practices. *Big Think +.* https://bigthink.com/plus/adult-learning-theory/

17. Sarah Schwartz (2023). Teacher Professional Development, Explained. *Education Week.* https://www.edweek.org/leadership/teacher-professional-development-explained/2023/07

18. Jana Hackathorn et al. (2011). All kidding aside: Humor increases learning at knowledge and comprehension levels. *Journal of the Scholarship of Teaching and Learning* 11, no. 4, pp. 116–123. https://files.eric.ed.gov/fulltext/EJ956757.pdf

19. Marc Marschark and R. Reed Hunt (1985). On memory and metaphor. Springer Link. https://link.springer.com/article/10.3758/BF03198454

1

Boosting Positive Energy

"I have so many mixed emotions about teaching. I enjoy aspects of my job but also find it hard to maintain my joy and energy throughout the day."

—Anonymous

When I started out my career in education, I was pretty darn excited about everything I'd learned in graduate school. I was armed with best practices! I was young! I was determined! I had positive energy! TGIM, people! I could have pushed over a small SUV with the superhuman strength I felt inside to Change. The. MF. World.

I vividly remember sitting in staff meetings, pencil poised above my notepad, ready to learn!

And I also remember noticing grouchy people, pencils down, ready to complain. What the heck was wrong with them?

Fast forward 10 years, and oh snap . . . *I* was the grouch. Maybe not on the outside to a casual observer, but on the inside. I had grown cynical. Slowly, I had begun drowning in the quicksand of negativity, anxious about the high expectations I could never meet, and demoralized at the grossly understaffed and under-resourced system I worked in. And each day, more and more tasks and roles were being added to my already full plate. Sound familiar?

(Oh! And if that doesn't sound familiar because you're brand new to the profession – don't freak out! You are in the lucky position to stop burnout before it even takes hold!)

Let's do a quick reflection to see how full your tank is.

On a scale of 1-10 with one being "I want to quit" and 10 being "TGIM! (Thank Goodness it's Monday!)," I am at a _____ with my positive energy level.

Why Filling Your Tank Is Essential

When you think of someone who is burned out, you might conjure up an image of someone just "phoning it in" and not caring about their job. That's not what burnout for educators and care professionals usually looks like. It often looks like *running on empty in overdrive.*

Passion can often lead to burnout.[1] Educators are the perfect example of passion-driven helping professionals, and thus they are more susceptible to burnout because they are surrounded by pressure to love the job. I experienced this firsthand, as a school psychologist bringing home my work every night and weekend because I cared so much. I was running on the fumes of my bigger why – my love for the students I served.[2] Chances are, you have done the same.

I could go into all the dangers of running on fumes in overdrive, and all the dangers of chronic stress. But chances are, you already know that high levels of stress or chronic stress is related to almost any negative outcome you can think of. If you want to freak yourself out, check out APA's 2023 Stress in America report, which paints a vivid picture of how stress is more than just an emotional burden: it's a physical one, too. Stress, often seen as a mental and emotional challenge, manifests physically, leading to conditions like heart disease and weakened immune systems. Particularly striking is the hidden toll of stress on those who appear resilient; they can show accelerated aging at the cellular level, a somber reminder that appearances can be deceiving, and that resilience can have a cost. This revelation underscores the need for more supportive environments in our schools, where educators' successes aren't at the expense of their own health.

The thing is, you can't typically control the stressors – high class sizes, high demands, increasing student needs – but you *can* control your mindset and reaction to the stressors.

I'm not saying that burnout is some sort of personal self-care fail. I'm not going to spout "cruel optimism" where we put the burden of change on the individual in a system where the stress cards are stacked against them. This book is about practical optimism. We absolutely need to work on upstream workplace issues like reducing class size, increasing mental health and learning supports, and giving educators more autonomy over bureaucracy. We also need to acknowledge that there are larger forces at work in our society that add stress upon stress, such as racism, sexism, ablism, and policy choices that adversely impact marginalized groups in our schools. But until we sort all those complex upstream challenges, what can we do on Monday? What is the fuel for a happy educator in challenging circumstances? Let's geek out on that.

Before we launch into the happiness fuel we need to thrive as educators, let's pause for a moment about the goal itself, of boosting positive emotions. Barbara Frederickson's research on happiness reveals that positive emotions are not just pleasant but necessary to be a functioning human! Engaging in activities that make us happy doesn't only improve our mood; it also enhances our creativity, problem-solving skills, and even our physical health. Happiness is not a "nice to have," it is a "need to have" for educators to thrive. Positive emotions both broaden and build our cognitive and emotional resources.[3]

Just look at Figure 1.1, showing all the correlates of happiness!

While we can all agree happiness is a worthy goal in and of itself, there are also many reasons to prioritize happiness as educators, as it also improves our craft and student outcomes. The double-edged sword of helping professionals is that we tend to be high achievers (great!) but we can also be a self-critical bunch (not so great). When a lesson bombs, an angry parent shows up with harsh words, or when a hard-to-reach student is giving us a hard time again, we often take it to heart.

With the barrage of daily stressors and "best-laid-plans short-falls," we often give our weaknesses and limitations more attention than our strengths. But research suggests that thinking about personal strengths can increase our happiness and reduce depression.[4]

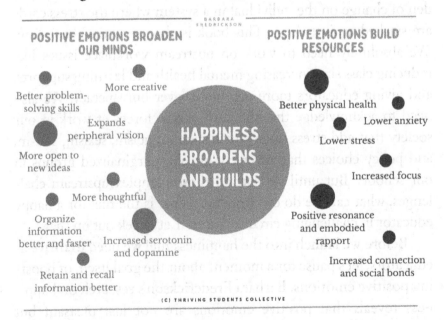

FIGURE 1.1 Broaden and Build Theory

While we shouldn't ignore our shortcomings, reflecting on our strengths can help remind us of our positive attributes, and this can build our confidence, self-efficacy, and self-esteem – and, in turn, increase happiness.

Research shows that using your strengths intentionally at work leads to greater overall satisfaction and makes mundane or frustrating tasks feel less burdensome.[5]

A recent study shows that people who have the opportunity to use their strengths are:[6]

- 7.8% more productive
- 6x as likely to strongly agree that they have the chance to do what they do best every day
- 6x more likely to be engaged at work

So how can we focus on our strengths? In one study, participants tried using a personal strength each day for one week. Compared with those who didn't try to use a strength – instead they wrote about their memories every day for a week – those who identified and used their strengths reported an increase in happiness and a decrease in symptoms of depression immediately after the one-week experiment, and those changes persisted six months later.[7]

Bridging the Research to Your Reality

Now the fun part! Let's translate that research into reality. What practical things can you do, during your day, to shift your lens from focusing on what's wrong to what's strong?

Know Your Strengths

Step one is knowing your strengths. When I present across the country and ask a room of educators what their strengths are, I am frequently met with blank stares. What typically follows is one reluctant participant raises their hand and offers, almost as if a question "I'm a good listener?" Another tentatively adds, "I am good at helping?" Even when I give teachers permission to brag a little, very few people feel comfortable sharing their strengths. Some have "strength blindness" altogether, where they've never really even thought to stop and think about what they're good at. Sometimes educators are so focused on their students' strengths, they forget to look at their own! If you took the Thrive-o-gram, now you're one of the small percentage of adults who know and can articulate their strengths! Now is a great time to pull it out as a reference so you can have your strengths at the forefront of your mind as you read this book. And if you haven't taken it yet, this is an optimal time to do that!

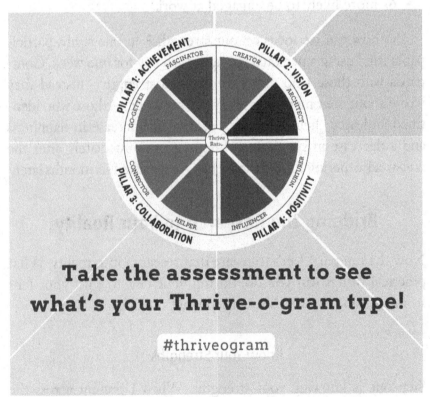

Take the assessment to see what's your Thrive-o-gram type!

#thriveogram

FIND OUT YOUR TYPE! THRIVINGSTUDENTS.COM/THRIVEOGRAM

Recognizing Flow in the Classroom

Have you ever felt so immersed in an activity that time seemed to vanish? This state, known as "flow," is not just a fleeting joy but a critical psychological state where you're at your most engaged and productive. Reflect on when you experience flow during your school day – those moments when joy in teaching makes time fly.

I am in flow when _____

Chances are, in these moments, you are using your strengths. This is your positive energy fuel!

Micromovements Toward Recharging

The key to sustainable energy isn't found in grand gestures and big chunks of time to rest, but in the small, consistent efforts to recharge. Like a car, it's easier to refuel a little at a time rather than stressing out when you're running on fumes and trying to find a bunch of time to refuel. Small, micromovements toward recharging will be far more effective than the elusive "big break."

Why is this important? Let me tell you a little tale about big stress vs. "microstressors."

Imagine you go to school tomorrow, and there's a huge altercation in your classroom. A child screams at you, throws his desk over, and you call the office for help and no one comes. You have to evacuate your whole classroom as the child is a danger to himself and others. When the situation finally calms down, you go on with your day, grateful no one was hurt. But then, at the end of the day, the child's parent comes in and yells at you for not being able to manage your classroom. Now that's a big stressful day!

Chances are, after a day like this, you'll go home and think of ways you can de-stress, whether it's having a big ol' cry on a friend's shoulder, working out, watching a distractingly funny show, or just taking the world's longest bubble bath. Maybe you even take a mental health day the next day to reset your nervous system. Big stress often results in self-care activation. You know you need to take care of yourself because the stress was undeniable.

Now, imagine another day, in which you have to work right until the bell rings because there was unexpected traffic. You don't have time to even set down your bag before kids come in your classroom. In your haste to get organized, you spill coffee on your favorite shirt. Throughout the day, there are a few annoyances, but nothing huge. The copier jams. You get a weird side eye from a colleague at lunch when you're talking about a lesson, but she doesn't say anything. You stub your toe at yard duty. And you get a curt email from a parent.

Chances are, after a day like this, you don't have a big ol' cry or activate some self-care mechanism. After all, this is par for the course. Of course there are tiny annoying things in your day. The thing is, your body accumulates all these "microstresses" just as it does a big stress. And unless you complete the stress cycle of activating self-care, it stays with you – in the back of your mind, and in your body, and it all adds up. As Cross & Dillon note in their article, "The Hidden Toll of Microstress," microstresses are so insidious because they slip past our defenses.[8] If you barely register the negativity in the moment, your normal stress response doesn't fire and the stress accrues.

And that, my friend, is why you must refuel and recharge a little every single day, whether you had one big stress or a bunch of microstressors!

Positive Priming – Setting the Stage for Success

Raise your hand if you like to be right! I personally love being right, who doesn't?!? While we don't always shout it like the character in the old Smurfs cartoon, Brainy Smurf, with his cry of "I was right!" we do get a little satisfaction, don't we? And guess what? Our brains love to be right, too. Our brains adore patterns, and when we prime ourselves with positivity, we are more likely to continue recognizing positive aspects in our lives. Our brains are constantly scanning for confirmation of our beliefs. If you believe you are underappreciated and nothing you do is right, the inner Brainy Smurf in your brain is going to lock in on those moments and declare (probably in an annoying voice), "Ha! I was right!" The fancy term for it is priming. Our beliefs prime our brains to scan for evidence that we are right.

Good news is that priming works for positivity, too. By visualizing positive outcomes and acknowledging our strengths, we set ourselves up for success, reducing stress and fostering resilience. It's like playing a strengths-based movie in your mind with a positive outcome. Have a tricky parent meeting coming up? Instead of playing out all the things that could go wrong and how bad it's going to be, harness your strengths. Love learning? Imagine all you will learn about diffusing parents. Is creativity your strength? Get creative about ways to connect with the family.

Get Energy from Your Students

One of the sources of energy is the kids themselves! For sure, they can also drain your energy, but that typically happens if you are giving, giving, giving all day. If you're doing all the talking, redirecting, organizing, and managing in the classroom, it can be exhausting. But what if you flipped the script and fed off their buzzing energy? What if you helped them channel their strengths into co-creating a vibrant classroom environment together?

One way to do this is to provide them with autonomy, ownership, and opportunities to tap into *their* strengths. Do you have a kid who is great at tech? She can have the classroom "job" of tech support for setting up your slides. One of your students excels at art? Ask for help with drawing the parts of a cell on the board. Are your out-of-the box and creative students complaining something is "boring?" Set up an area of the classroom where they can go to quietly work on the topic in a novel way. Maybe you're studying Ancient Rome, and they could create a model of the Coliseum, or they could research a famous Roman and imagine what their social media profile would look like today. Turn that creative energy into engaged learning!

Another way to get energy from your students is to build in time to bond and have fun together. Take 10 minutes at the beginning of every class and do something fun. It can be anything! Show them a funny music video from when you were a kid and ask them what they think. Have a fun question of the day as you take attendance. Welcome them in the class with a high-five or special greeting. Anything that would be fun for you and your students builds connection. And connection fuels engagement. So rather than pouring everything you have into your students and then having to take a break from them to refuel, you can fill up each other's positive energy tanks with fun rituals, having them use their strengths, and building community together.

Blend Work with Passion

One of the genius strategies from Angela Watson, my co-creator of *How to Reverse Educator Burnout*, is to make the conscious distinction between work-work and hobby work.

Long gone are the days of the 1950s "punch clock" when your work hours ended when you punched a timecard, went home, and you were done with work until you showed up the next day to punch in. Now, our work follows us home, in the form of unanswered emails, to-dos we didn't get to, and a culture of "you are always on the job."

Not all work you bring home is the same. Some tasks you bring home at the end of the day are like sipping a warm cup of tea on a rainy day – enjoyable and comforting. Others? More like trudging through a downpour without an umbrella. Recognizing this difference is key to managing your energy and enthusiasm.

Now, let's talk about those energizing activities you do in your downtime. Imagine cozying up on a weekend evening, diving into the online world of lesson planning, or crafting teaching resources while your favorite show plays in the background. These tasks are fun and might not feel like work. They're done out of pure passion, with no looming deadlines. It's not an every-night affair, but when it happens, it's fun, right? There's no need to set boundaries on these moments of inspiration. Let them be a free-flowing source of joy, a wellspring of ideas that makes you look forward to your time in the classroom.

But then there's the obligatory work – the stuff that feels like a chore. We've all been there: dragging home those papers to grade, that report to write, or forms to complete, wishing we could just leave them at school. It's a whole different ballgame from those relaxing Pinterest binges. That's why it's crucial to draw a line in the sand. Allocate a specific chunk of time and self-imposed boundaries for these must-dos.

Micro-Habits to Use Your Thrive-O-Gram Strengths

To tap into your strengths, we are going to use the micro-habit of affirmations. Habit formation research shows that when we pair a new habit with a well-established one, we are more likely to do the new habit. Therefore, pairing affirmations with automatic activities, such as drinking a morning cup of coffee, brushing teeth, or buckling a seatbelt on the way to work, can reinforce our strengths. Or maybe you change your password to something that includes your strength so you are constantly reminded of it! As we learned in the introduction, our brains love to be "right."

If we tell ourselves each morning, or when we type our password, that we are strong and capable, our brains will scan our day for confirmation of this to be "right." It's like putting on strengths-colored glasses; we will start to prime ourselves for opportunities in the day to make it happen.

Here's a fun way to remember this. Ever see the old *Saturday Night Live* sketch with "Stuart Smalley?" If not, it's worth a quick search to watch an old clip. In the bit, he gets people like Michael Jordan to look in the mirror and tell themselves positive affirmations. The gag is you *know* that these folks tell themselves this already, and that this positive mindset is part of their success. It's quite funny to watch superstars repeat: "I'm good enough, smart enough, and doggone it, people like me!" Now, it's your turn!

Keep in mind, that the following suggestions are based on your Thrive-o-gram strengths profile, but we often have multiple strengths. You can look at only your profile if you want to focus on one idea, or you can choose from any of the suggestions that resonate with you. The best strategy is the one that you try that works for you!

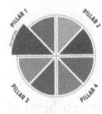 **Go-Getter:** Challenge yourself to 30 days of self-affirmations and track it on your planner. At the beginning of each day, when creating your to-do list, write down your affirmation before crushing that to-do list!

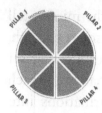

Fascinator: Research strengths-based assessments for yourself and your students. For example, check out Via Character strengths or Clifton-Strengths finder. Fascinate yourself with your strengths and how to bring them out in others.

Creator: In addition to repeating your own strengths, consider creating an activity for students to do the same. Create an affirmation mirror where students enter the class and share their strength. Have your students make a strengths card or word art on their desks to reference daily. Get creative!

Architect: Is there a systems-wide affirmation intervention you can do with your colleagues and/or students? Think about ways you can integrate strengths into the vision of your school culture. A "Know Your Strengths" awareness campaign? Strengths week? Staff meeting affirmation rituals? Think big, architect!

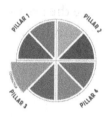

Connector: Buddy up with a favorite colleague and share your strengths with one another. Using your strengths, create a plan to build an affirmation ritual in your day (for you and your students!). Teamwork makes the dream work, right?

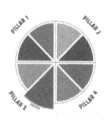

Helper: One of your core strengths is kindness, so can you come up with a way to be kind to yourself with ritualizing a positive self-affirmation each day? Since you love to help too, think of a way you can encourage your students to use positive and kind self-talk in the classroom. Modeling kindness is a great way to help others!

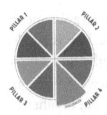

Influencer: When you look in the mirror, tell yourself you're good enough, smart enough, and, doggone it, you are a leader! Leaders set a good example, so practice what you preach and bring strength-based affirmations into your classroom and model it for the students.

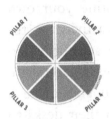

Nurturer: You'll probably love self-affirmations, since one of your core strengths is self-awareness! Pick a daily ritual that reminds you of this strength, such as journaling or creating a visual reminder of your positive affirmation.

Your Thriving Road Map

As we conclude this first leg on our Thriving Journey, remember that your journey to "Thrive Town" is not just about maintaining a full tank; it's about having a surplus of strengths-based fuel to give abundantly and in the long haul without depletion. Being an educator requires daily refueling, and your strengths are the greatest source of fuel there is. No more running on empty in overdrive!

Write down one micro-habit strategy from this chapter that you want to take with you as a souvenir for yourself.

Write down one micro-habit strategy from this chapter that you want to take with you as a souvenir to use at your school or with your students.

Discussion Questions:

1. **Mixed Emotions in Teaching:** The text begins with an educator expressing mixed emotions about their job, enjoying aspects of it but also struggling to maintain joy and energy. How do you relate to these feelings, and what strategies do you use to balance the joys and challenges of teaching?

2. **Preventing Burnout:** The author discusses the susceptibility of passionate educators to burnout due to the nature of their job and societal pressures. What beliefs do you hold that may be unintentionally fueling burnout? What are some new beliefs that you might be able to start using to shift your mindset about what it takes to be a successful educator?

3. **Mindset and Reaction to Stressors:** According to the text, while educators can't always control the stressors, they can control their mindset and reaction. How do you cultivate a positive mindset even under stressful circumstances? Do you have a personal mantra that has been helpful to you?

4. **Role of Positive Emotions:** The author emphasizes the significance of positive emotions in enhancing creativity, problem-solving skills, and physical health. Discuss how fostering positive emotions in the classroom can impact both teachers and student outcomes.

5. **Strengths-Focused Approach:** Research suggests focusing on personal strengths can increase happiness and reduce depression. What was your Thrive-o-gram strength? Did your profile resonate with you?

6. Your Personal Road Map: Using your Thriving Road Map from Appendix A as a guide, what is one action step you can take immediately to use your strengths? What were your "souvenir" ideas you want to share with students?

Notes

1. Jennifer Moss (2019). When Passion Leads to Burnout. *Harvard Business Review*. https://hbr.org/2019/07/when-passion-leads-to-burnout.
2. Jennifer Moss (2019). When Passion Leads to Burnout. *Harvard Business Review*. https://hbr.org/2019/07/when-passion-leads-to-burnout.
3. Barbara L. Fredrickson (2001). The Role of Positive Emotions in Positive Psychology: The Broaden-and-Build Theory of Positive Emotions. *American Psychologist* 56, no. 3, pp. 218–226. https://doi.org/10.1037/0003-066X.56.3.218
4. CliftonStrengths (2024). How to Improve Your Career Development. *Gallup.* https://www.gallup.com/cliftonstrengths/en/299855/how-to-improve-my-career.aspx?utm_source=cliftonstrengths&utm_medium=email&utm_campaign=meaningful_conversations_email_2_november_11182023&utm_term=store&utm_content=using_your_strengths_intentionally_at_work_textlink_1
5. CliftonStrengths (2024). How to Improve Your Career Development. *Gallup.* https://www.gallup.com/cliftonstrengths/en/299855/how-to-improve-my-career.aspx?utm_source=cliftonstrengths&utm_medium=email&utm_campaign=meaningful_conversations_email_2_november_11182023&utm_term=store&utm_content=using_your_strengths_intentionally_at_work_textlink_1
6. CliftonStrengths (2024). How to Improve Your Career Development. *Gallup.* https://www.gallup.com/cliftonstrengths/en/299855/how-to-improve-my-career.aspx?utm_source=cliftonstrengths&utm_medium=email&utm_campaign=meaningful_conversations_email_2_november_11182023&utm_term=store&utm_content=using_your_strengths_intentionally_at_work_textlink_1
7. M. E. P. Seligman, T. A. Steen, N. Park, and C. Peterson (2005). Positive Psychology Progress: Empirical Validation of Interventions. *American Psychologist* 60, no. 5, pp. 410–421. https://doi.org/10.1037/0003-066X.60.5.410
8. Rob Cross and Karen Dillon (2024). The Hidden Toll of Microstress. *Harvard Business Review*, Special Issue, Spring 2024, pp. 10-18

CHAPTER

2

Cultivate Work-Life Balance

"I can't be inbox zero, laundry zero, dishes zero, *and* find time to take care of myself, my family, and all my students at the same time. There's just not enough time in the day."

—Caroline, 5th grade teacher

In this chapter, we delve into the second step in our journey to Thrive Town, the elusive goal of "work-life balance." Before we do, I hate to break it to you, but . . . *Work-life balance is a joke.*

It is practically impossible. There's no world in which you can give equally to each part of your life all the time. Balance is never something you can achieve once and for all, because life is constantly changing. When we try to achieve "perfect" balance, we get stressed because we're trying to make everything come out equal when it's just not.

I'm sure you've had this experience. You tell yourself you need better work-life balance, so you decide you are definitely not taking work home. Then you're sitting at home worrying about work and not getting everything done, so you're not really enjoying your downtime. Or, you might have a big project at work and stay late, and then you feel guilty because you "should" be at home, enjoying your downtime with friends and family. Either way, you are not present. When you are at work, you're thinking about home, and when you're at home, you're thinking about work.

That's why I like to talk about work-life *alliance* instead. Like the tires on our car, we need to keep them in alignment and be mindful when we are out of alignment and pulling too much toward work. The goal is not dividing up our time 50/50 and rigidly trying to stick with it. It's about mindfully and actively balancing or staying in alignment, adjusting depending on the situation.

Why Work-Life Balance Is Essential for Burnout Prevention

Work-life balance, or rather work-life *alliance*, is important because spending too many hours working can lead to chronic stress, which weakens the immune system and makes us more susceptible to illness and burnout. Maintaining a healthy work-life balance protects our health and energy levels.

I remember when I first started out as a school psychologist, I worked all the time to try to keep up with my insane workload. Every night and every weekend, I was writing reports and turning down fun things with my friends to "catch up." This "always on" mindset stressed me out, but I felt like I *had to*, because there was work to be done and deadlines to meet. Oh, what I wouldn't give to time travel back then and tell myself that enjoying my personal life would actually fuel my focus, productivity, and creativity at work (and not to mention reduce my overall stress and improve my well-being!).

Friends, hear me out: Time is not a renewable resource. You can always work, but you can't get your free time back to enjoy your friends, family, and your personal life!

Bridging the Research to Your Reality

Here's the kicker – we typically know, deep down, when we are out of balance or alignment, but we don't necessarily know what to do about it. So, let's translate research into reality. What are practical things you can do to achieve more balance?

Recognizing Early Warning Signs

Let's start by understanding the importance of early warning signs, drawing parallels from a real-life (and sort of embarrassing) story. One day, I was driving and saw my car alert me that my tire pressure was low, and I should stop to get them checked. The alert also read: "*If you have run-flat tires, you can continue at speeds up to 50 miles per hour.*" So, not even knowing if I had these magical run-flat tires or not, I ignored the alert, thinking, "Great! I can keep going! I have a lot of errands to run." And then a wise person in the car (my then 8-year-old daughter) said, "Mommy, we should just stop and take care of it, so we don't get in an accident." She was, of course, right. So, we found a tire store, and it literally took 10 minutes to pump them back up and we were off, safe and sound, no worries or potential accident lurking (p.s. I did not have run-flat tires!).

Just like ignoring a car's warning light can lead to trouble, ignoring our personal warning signs of burnout can leave us metaphorically stranded. So, take a moment to think about your cues for feeling out of balance. Identifying these signs early on is essential to realign ourselves and prevent stress from taking over. For some people, an early warning sign of being out of balance is general crankiness and irritability. Maybe it's trouble sleeping, over-eating sugary foods or drinking caffeinated beverages, or under-eating because you don't have time for lunch. Take a moment to think of your early warning sign that you are out of balance and write it below.

My early warning sign I'm out of balance is: _____

The Myth of Perfect Balance

Understanding that perfect work-life balance is a myth is crucial. Striving for a work-life *alliance*, aligned with our personal values, is more realistic and rewarding than the stress of pulling ourselves in separate directions, or trying the impossible task of giving equal attention to competing high priorities at both home and at work.

So, what is the research behind this strategy? We can turn to the principles of Acceptance and Commitment Therapy (ACT), which teaches us to align our actions with our values rather than avoiding or denying our feelings. This alignment helps decrease depression, anxiety, workplace stress, and even chronic pain.[1]

One practical way to realign your behavior with your values is by asking yourself, "Where does my energy need to be right now?" Sometimes, we need to put more energy into our work because it's crunch time. Sometimes, we need to pull back from work to put more energy into our families, because we have an aging parent, a child who needs some extra TLC, or a partner who we are feeling disconnected from. And yet other times, we have gone the proverbial 50 miles per hour on run-flat tires that are bald and about to pop and we really need to put energy into ourselves and pull over for a break to refuel (see Chapter 1) and get back in alignment ourselves.

So, the next time you're out of balance, reflect on where your energy needs to be focused. Whether it's work, family, or personal time, being in flow with your energy needs and accepting where you are at the moment can greatly enhance your sense of well-being.

Strategic Stopping: The Power of Pause

One effective strategy to maintain this alliance is strategic stopping. It involves pausing an activity before we become tired, thus allowing us to return to it later with renewed energy and less resentment. Research shows that this approach of stopping while ahead can significantly enhance our productivity and well-being when trying to complete mentally demanding tasks.[2]

So, what does this look like on a practical level? Imagine you have a stack of papers to grade, a lesson to plan, or some mundane report you need to complete. Monitor your energy level as you tackle this project, and when you start to feel like you're running out of steam, instead of pushing through, stop. Tell yourself, "I will be able to complete this task more efficiently when I am rested." The key is to not wait until you feel tired or annoyed and are generally now in a bad mood as you do the task. Tackle part of it, and then return with a positive attitude (remember from Chapter 1 that positive mood enhances our cognitive skills?).

Language and Choice: Shifting from Should to Could

When we shift our mindsets, we shift our behavior. What exactly do I mean by a mindset? Mindsets are implicit beliefs that we are often not even consciously aware of that color our world and often guide us to make decisions. For example, if you have the belief in a relationship that "absence makes the heart grow fonder" you are going to be much more positive about a partner taking a work trip for a month than if you hold the belief, "out of sight, out of mind." The reality is the same – your partner is leaving – but how you react will change based on your mindset.

In our work as educators, one of the most common mindsets that can get us in trouble with work-life alliance is this: "I *should* bring this work home to get caught up" or "I *should* stay at work until this is done." This is a mindset trap. The reality is that when you are an educator, the work is never done and you will never be caught up, because *kids are never done*. Thus, by the communitive property of burnout (which I just made up right now) if you work until you are done *you will never stop working*.

A simple yet powerful habit hack to combat this tendency to over-work involves changing our language from "should" to "could." This shift can transform our sense of control and choice, empowering us to make decisions that align with our values and current priorities. It's a big difference between "I *should* bring home this stack of papers over the weekend" and "I *could* bring home this stack of papers over the weekend." Whether you bring them home or not isn't good or bad, it's about making a mindful, conscious choice.

Micro-Habits to Use Your Thrive-O-Gram Strength

To tap into your strengths, we are going to use the micro-habit of using intentional language and "catching yourself" if you find yourself silently judging yourself based on your mindset about work-life balance and what you "should" do with your time. Ask yourself throughout the day "Am I doing this because I *want to* or because I feel I *should*?" If it's because you "should," then ask yourself "Why do I think I should?" or "What am I afraid will happen if I don't do it?" That can help you get to the underlying implicit belief that might be subconsciously driving your behavior.

As my good friend, Angela Watson, shares in our course:

Don't make judgments about yourself regarding what's important for your alignment. Never ignore an area because you feel like you "shouldn't" value it as much as you do, or pressure yourself to incorporate self-care practices that don't matter to you, simply because you feel like they "should" make the list. Alignment is about identifying what YOU need to thrive, and that's an individual thing.

Here's a fun way (albeit a little crass – forgive me!) to remember this concept: Albert Ellis was a famous psychologist who advocated the importance of accepting yourself just because you are alive, human, and unique – and not judging yourself based on what you "should" do, or being influenced by what others think you "should" do. He famously said, "Stop 'shoulding' on yourself." If you prefer a less crass adage, you can tap into what one of my students once told me when I asked what he planned to do on the weekend, and he responded with: "*Imma do me.*" Wise words from the youth: You do you!

Now it's time to find a strategy that works for you! Check out the following suggestions for work-life alliance based on your Thrive-o-gram strengths profile. You *could* also choose from any of the suggestions that look fun to try from the other profiles. Remember that the "best" strategy is the one you choose. It's like a souvenir on the trip to Thrive Town that you can bring with you that you think will work in your context.

Go-Getter: As someone who loves to-do lists, it might be hard for you to not think about your list when you are at home. If you find yourself ruminating or over-thinking about what you must do tomorrow, give yourself a set "think time." Set a timer for 10 minutes to think about your to-do list and then pivot to an enjoyable activity (preferably one that is incompatible with thinking about work, like reading a book for fun, watching a show, socializing, or taking a class where you have to focus on something else).

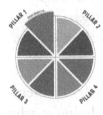

Fascinator: One of your burnout traps is that you are fascinated by learning so many different things, you might go down a rabbit hole after work to find the perfect activity, a new way to teach something, or delve into over-planning. Give yourself a "stop time" on your work and be intentional about your language. Instead of "I *should* redo my slides" you could say, "I *get to* redo my slides if that feels fun to me" or "I *choose to* fix my slides for 30 minutes and then stop."

Creator: A creative mind is always jamming! That's why it's hard sometimes to shut it down, am I right? You *could* (not should!) find a way to set time limits for thinking about work if work thoughts are interfering with your down time balance. One way to do this is writing down your intentions for the evening after work, like, "I can think about work until dinner time and then I can shift to relax mode."

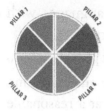

Architect: One way you *could* (not should!) be more mindful of your work-life alliance is to analyze your calendar. Consider color coding your events by priority – self time, work time, family time, etc. and see if the balance seems right to you. If not, make strategic adjustments by calendaring out your priorities just like you would an important meeting.

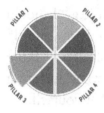

Connector: Practice the buddy system! For example, if you want to be more in alignment with a need for exercise, ask a colleague to take a walk over lunch or after school, do a 10K steps challenge with you, or sign up for an exercise class with a friend and keep each other accountable.

Helper: One of the burnout traps of the helper profile is putting your own needs on the back burner to help others. Of the zillions of things you do to help others, each day balance one helping activity for others with one activity that is restorative for your energy. For example, if you love theater and you volunteer with helping after school with the school musical, also take time to go to the theater yourself or participate in a community theater program for adults (if that is fun for you!). "One for me, one for you" is a motto you can use to keep in balance.

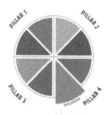

Influencer: One of your strengths is leading by example. When you are excited about the prospect of fostering a healthy work-life alliance for yourself, you can inspire your colleagues to do the same. Share your favorite research to reality strategy (e.g. strategic stopping, should vs. could language) with others and get a discussion started!

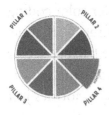

Nurturer: Like the helper, you likely are very good at giving amazing advice and nurturing wisdom to others to go home at a reasonable time and take time for themselves. But then, maybe you don't give yourself the same level of self-compassion? In these moments, check the message you are telling yourself (e.g. "I should finish this before I go home") and ask yourself, "would I give this advice to a colleague?" If the answer is no, then ask yourself what nurturing advice you would give and do that yourself!

Your Thriving Road Map

As we conclude this leg of our Thriving Journey, remember one of my favorite mindfulness phrases, "Be where your feet are." Whether at work or home, being present in the moment and focusing your energy where it's needed can help achieve a work-life alliance.

Write down one micro-habit strategy from this chapter that you want to take with you as a souvenir for yourself.

Write down one micro-habit strategy from this chapter that you want to take with you as a souvenir to use at your school or with your students.

Discussion Questions:

1. **Aligning Actions with Values:** The chapter discusses the concept of work-life alliance as an alternative to work-life balance. List your top three values – both personally and professionally, such as making time for family, prioritizing your mental and physical health, inspiring students to love learning, striving for excellence in teaching, etc. How can you align your daily actions with your core personal and professional values, and what would that alignment look like in practice for you?

2. **Recognizing Early Burnout Signs:** The author uses the metaphor of a car's warning light for recognizing early signs of burnout. Reflect on a time when you noticed such a warning sign in your own professional life. How did you address it? Or did you ignore it? What happened? Pick one early warning sign and what you could do when you see it to prevent being "stranded" by burnout in the future.

3. **Shifting from "Should" to "Could":** The chapter advises changing your language from "should" to "could" to transform our sense of control and choice. How could this shift in language and perspective change the way you approach your workload and self-care practices?

4. **Strategic Stopping and the Power of Pause:** Strategic stopping is recommended to avoid exhaustion. Discuss a time

when you benefited from taking a pause in your work, and how implementing regular "strategic stops" might impact your teaching and personal well-being.

5. **Reflecting on Personal Energy Needs:** Considering the idea that our energy needs may shift between work, family, or personal time, discuss how reflecting on and honoring these shifting needs can lead to a better work-life alliance. What strategies or "micro-habits" might you develop to ensure you're giving attention to where it's needed most at any given time?

6. **Your Personal Road Map:** Using your Thriving Road Map from Appendix A as a guide, what is one action step you can take immediately to cultivate more work-life alliance? What were your "souvenir" ideas you want to share with students?

Notes

1. Zhihing Li et al. (2022). Characteristics and trends in acceptance and commitment therapy research. *Front. Psychol.* https://www.ncbi.nlm.nih .gov/pmc/articles/PMC9702511/
2. Gerhard Blasche et al. (2018). Comparison of rest-break interventions during a mentally demanding task. Stress Health. https://www.ncbi.nlm .nih.gov/pmc/articles/PMC6585675/

CHAPTER

3

Build a Support Network

"We are not meant to do this work alone."
—Mona, Rural School Psychologist

In this chapter, we're embarking on a vital part of our journey to Thrive Town – building a support network. Having delved into boosting positive energy and cultivating work-life balance, we now turn our focus to one of the most critical aspects of thriving as educators and mental health professionals – building a support network both in and out of work.

Let's start with some reflection. How do you feel after a staff meeting? This simple question can reveal a lot about the energy in your professional environment and the kind of support you might need.

After a staff meeting, I feel _____.

When I ask this question in professional development trainings with educators around the world, sadly, the answers typically tend to skew toward the negative – words like "exhausted," "annoyed," "overwhelmed," and even "demoralized." That being said, some folks feel "energized" and "happy" after meeting with colleagues. Your personal answer to this question can say a lot about the culture of your school and the energetic milieu you are in!

Why We Need to Build a Support Network

Rarely is there one thing that helps everyone with stress, but guess what? Scientists have found something pretty darn close. Turns out, social support works for *everyone* to combat stress.[1] Strong social bonds are like a balm for stress-related ailments, from preventing depression and heart disease to even cutting the risk of early death *by half*.[2] This is a crucial takeaway for educators and mental health providers and support staff in the schools, who not only need to protect themselves from stress, but also play a pivotal role in fostering these connections within the school community.

Research from the 2023 APA study shows that strong social bonds can help protect us from the negative effects of stress. But finding positive support as an educator is often easier said than done, especially if your school climate is negative, you have an itinerant role, are in a rural setting, or are isolated in your classroom all day without any colleagues. Being an educator can mean that even though you are surrounded by humans all day (some tiny, some adults), you can still feel isolated.

I remember that when I worked in a large urban school district as a school psychologist, it was so rare to interface with my school psychologist colleagues, except at monthly staff meetings at the district office. At these meetings, when I'd see a like-minded and positive school psychologist colleague, it was like seeing the first person since the apocalypse! I would mentally declare, "OMG! There's another one! It's going to all be okay!"

We don't just need people. We need *our* people. We need supportive people. Buckle up for a whole lot of research about the power of support networks.

Bridging the Research to Your Reality

In this section, I will share the research on social support and offer practical strategies for choosing your "passengers" wisely on this journey to Thrive Town. Who you surround yourself with can significantly impact your ability to stay motivated and uplifted when facing challenges. In both your professional and personal life, it's important to build and maintain a supportive network. And it's not just about avoiding negativity, but also actively fostering positivity and resilience by garnering strategic support.

The Power of Emotional Contagion

As a school psychologist who often had several school placements, I've noticed that different schools can have remarkably different energies. In one school, when you walk in, you feel a sense of belonging and comradery. In another, you feel a sense of isolation and emotional toxicity. Why is that? It's biology, and a concept called "emotional contagion."

Research shows that as humans, we're equipped with mirror neurons that detect and copy each other's moods, making us susceptible to the emotional climate around us.[3] This makes sense from an evolutionary standpoint – to survive, we need to be able to detect if someone is a threat or an ally, and we need to be able to adapt to situations. The spooky sci-fi part of it though, is that this process of detecting and copying each others' moods is unconscious and happens in a matter of *milliseconds*.

Shawn Achor is a brilliant positive psychology author who outlines this subterranean process, and why it impacts our moods, in his book, *The Happiness Advantage*. He notes:[4]

- We can detect the mood in another in .33 milliseconds
- In about that same amount of time, we are subconsciously primed to emulate that mood
- When three strangers enter a room, the most emotionally expressive person can influence the moods of the others in just two minutes!

You know the vibe. Perhaps you have a parent-teacher conference, and when you walk into the room and meet a parent for the first time, you can instantly sense if they are irritated, anxious and uncomfortable, or excited to be there, without them even saying a word. Then, you get irritated because they're irritated, anxious about saying the wrong thing, or you sense their excitement and then get excited to meet them.

This phenomenon is also the reason you can walk into one teacher's classroom and feel an immediate sense of ease and joy, and then pop down the hall to another teacher's classroom and feel agitated and uncomfortable. We're emotional sponges. This empathic response is sometimes a gift: we can bring our calm to chaos and co-regulate those around us because they begin to match our positive emotions. But it can also be a curse, if we aren't careful around people who repeatedly trigger that negative response.

What this all means is that emotions are contagious, and the moods of those we spend time with can significantly impact our stress levels. And this process is all subterranean (until now!).

Armed with this knowledge, you can consciously note the dynamic and choose a different reaction.

Be the Energy in the Room

A key habit hack I love is the mantra: "Don't adapt to the energy in the room; be the energy in the room." This mantra empowers us to shift the mood in a room, whether it's a staff meeting or a parent-teacher conference, by being a positive presence. Given that a person's mood can influence group dynamics in just two minutes, the first person to speak in a meeting becomes vital in setting any meeting's tone.

So, if a principal walks in and hurriedly declares, "Okay, I have bus duty in 30 minutes so let's get this done" the tone is that the meeting is an annoyance and perhaps perfunctory and the members of the group will strive to end the meeting as quickly as possible. If you come in and excitedly declare: "I'm glad we're meeting today to talk about how Johnny learns best and ways we can support him!" then the tone is positive and focused on garnering supports for the child, and chances are, the team will pick up on this and strive to keep things positive. This is an empowering idea, as it underscores the power of bringing positive energy to interactions, as we have the capacity to influence the entire mood of a group!

Be the Marigold

Jennifer Gonzales, one of my favorite teacher bloggers, has a genius metaphor to describe this phenomenon of surrounding yourself with people who uplift you and protecting yourself from negativity at school. In an article from her *Cult of Pedagogy* blog called "Find Your Marigold: The One Essential Rule for New Teachers," she observes that schools are filled with folks who either inspire positivity or spew toxicity.[5] She calls these individuals "marigolds" and "walnuts."

Apparently, people who garden know to plant marigolds around their plants because these sunny blooms both protect other plants from pests and harmful weeds and help whatever is around them to flourish. There are "marigolds" in our schools, too – these are the folks who are positive, supportive, and encouraging. They will help you flourish and ward off bad energy. I'll bet you can already conjure up a few people at your school who are "marigolds." If you feel excited, safe, and encouraged about the future of education when you are around them, or they are experts at helping you shake off the hideous awful-meeting ick, chances are, they are one of your protective marigolds.

On the flip side, gardeners know that you never plant a garden by a walnut tree. Turns out, walnuts give off a toxic substance that kills basically anything around them! In schools, these walnut individuals have a negative take on the administration, the kids, new initiatives, parents – you name it. In the blog, Jennifer points out that if you feel discouraged, overwhelmed, insecure, or embarrassed around them, chances are they are a walnut. I'll bet you can, off the top of your head, immediately conjure up who the serious walnut energy folks are at your school.

Of course, we humans all have marigold-y moments and walnut-y moments, and rarely are we exclusively one or the other all the time. Additionally, we can certainly have empathy for walnut people, as they are likely suffering in some way. Some may be in full-on burnout mode and need serious support. Your instinct to help may kick in, and maybe you want to be that support. If you are feeling extra marigold-y, you can certainly lend an empathic ear here and there. BUT, if it becomes taxing to engage every day with this individual, I encourage you to remember your bigger-picture dream and the vision you have for yourself and the students you serve. Does this person help you with your positive vision or drain you? Then, remember this too: To protect your positivity, you must protect your positive energy.

To whatever degree possible, find your marigolds and avoid the walnuts. Because if you don't, then you will start to absorb negative energy and you will lose sight of (and possibly hope for) your positive vision for the future of your career. Trust me, I speak from experience. When I started out in my first job, I was the Queen of Marigolds. Everything! Was! Awesome! I'd look around at the grouchy faces of school psychologists at staff meetings and I couldn't fathom how some school psychologists were so negative. What was their problem? That would never be me!

Years later, at the height of my burnout, I was the one with the grouchy walnut face at staff meetings. I had, slowly but surely, morphed into a walnut I barely recognized. Yikes. What can be done to harness marigold energy and put on your "psychological hazmat suit" to protect you from walnut energy?

The Power of 2 Plus 3

Interestingly, research from the Green Cross Academy of Traumatology shows that having just two supportive people at work can protect you from burnout.[6] These connections can be both informal and professional, but what matters is their ability to uplift and support you.

So, you've learned that the bad news is that toxic moods are contagious. Walnut energy is *highly* contagious. And the reality is, at some point in your career you may be assigned to a school with a toxic culture. Or more likely, you might have a handful of people in your school who are your walnuts. Even worse (for my Harry Potter fans out there), there may be one particularly negative person – a "positive emotional energy Dementor," sucking out all that is good and happy in you. Sadly, if one of those people is someone you must be in close contact with (like your boss, principal, or special education team member), you might find their negativity rubbing off on you on a daily basis. So, what can you do? Avoid them like the plague? Continue to get your life force sucked out of you?

I propose another option – that you put on a "psychological hazmat suit." Protect yourself.

First, if possible, limit your contact with this person. Don't hang out with them in the teacher's lounge or in the halls. If that's not possible, at least limit your engagement with them, especially when your own marigold energy is low. Engage when you have some extra marigold energy to spare, but before you do so, make sure you set your walnut energy deflector to "stun." One way I do this is when a person comes to me and starts venting but I'm already drained, I give empathy and then put boundaries on the time by saying something like, "That does sound hard. I'm sorry but I only have about five minutes to chat about this, because I have to call a parent/go to the copier/prep for my next class." Another strategy is to cite a mantra in your head that helps you remember that you do not have to engage or absorb their negativity. Phrases like "Not my circus, not my monkeys" or "Her feelings are hers, mine are mine" can be great circuit breakers in your body's natural tendency to mirror their feelings. Or, if you like visualizations, as the person is speaking, you can mentally put yourself on a beach and them on an island, so you have psychological distance from their energy.

Next, have compassion for the walnuts. Be curious, not judgmental, about why they are acting the way they are. Give them the most generous explanation you can think of to soften your judgments, because there could easily be a situational factor at play. Maybe their mom just died. Perhaps they have health issues they haven't shared with anyone, and they aren't feeling well. Maybe they are putting in 60-hour work weeks and are sleep deprived. Or maybe, they feel insecure about their teaching, so it's safer to blame the kids, parents, you, or the administration when a child is not doing well.

Lastly, as Jennifer suggests in her blog post, surround yourself with marigolds to "detox" from the walnuts. See, the good news is that (as we learned from our spooky sci-fi lesson about mirror neurons earlier in this chapter), *positivity is also contagious.* You can always reboot that positivity by consciously planting a garden of marigolds around you – both in and out of your school building. Remember, you only need *two* people at work who will be highly supportive when you are called upon to protect yourself. Surely you can find two "marigolds" at work!

The power of positive relationships also extends beyond the four walls of your school building. The Green Cross research on burnout prevention points to having two positive work colleagues and three people outside of work whom you can go to for support.[7] These people can be friends, family, therapists, nail salon technicians, your Zumba teacher, furry friends, other educators – really anyone who you would say is a marigold! The key is asking yourself how you feel after being around people in your life. If the answer is "supported," then they are a marigold!

This is the power of two plus three. Reflect on who those two work besties and three personal supporters are for you! (And maybe ask them out to lunch this week!)

Micro-Habits to Use Your Thrive-O-Gram Strength

It's habit hack time! Did you know that just being around another person can make our goals seem more achievable? You know the vibe. It's way easier to get to the gym, run that annoying errand, or finish that work project when you have a buddy. Thus, it's essential to identify who these supportive individuals are in both your work and personal life to keep you reaching for your goals.

Here's a fun study that demonstrates how social support helps when we encounter hurdles. Participants at the bottom of a hill were asked to judge the steepness, with or without a person nearby. When a friend was present, or even when participants merely thought of a supportive significant other, a steep hill was judged to be less steep. "This suggests that people rely on close others when considering how difficult tackling a given environment might be," says lead author Simone Schnall.[8]

How can you cultivate supportive networks to help *you* through life's steep hills and hurdles? Check out the following suggestions, based on your Thrive-o-gram strengths profile. Grab your favorite souvenir on the trip to Thrive Town!

 **Go-Getter:** Love making lists? Get out a piece of paper with two columns and write down all the "marigolds" in your work and in your life. Circle one at work and one in your personal life that you can strategically spend more time with. Make an "appointment" with each of them as a to-do item this week!

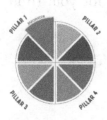 **Fascinator:** You love to learn and dive deep, so why not learn more about your colleagues? Bond with colleagues over shared interests outside of work. You might find out that a fellow teacher loves Bollywood dance class, or your principal is also a big *Star Wars* fan or has an interesting hobby. This creates a deeper connection and provides alternative topics for conversation, steering away from constant venting about work.

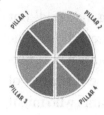

Creator: Get creative about protecting your energy. Visualize a barrier between yourself and energy-draining colleagues, like a limo partition or sitting far away in a bus. This mental image can help you maintain your positive energy and focus.

Architect: Take some data on how you feel after interactions with certain colleagues or people in your personal life. How marigold-y are they, from 1–10? Make strategic adjustments to spend more time with the most marigold-y of marigold friends and co-workers!

Connector: You are already quite skilled at practicing the buddy system! Be clear with your friends about the kind of support you need from them. Whether it's just listening or helping find solutions, communicating your needs helps them support you effectively. Nothing is worse than someone hopping in with a suggestion when all you want is an empathetic ear to just hear you out and empathize.

Helper: Your educator friends might come to you to be a positive helping source of marigold energy. This can lead to them dumping or venting with you because you are a good listener. To protect your energy, establish a rule for limiting school-related venting during social gatherings. Set a specific time for discussing work issues (we get to vent for 10 minutes!) and then consciously shift to other topics.

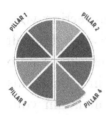

Influencer: You were born to be a marigold! But be sure to recharge yourself! Select fellow influencer educators to be part of your support network. They understand the unique challenges of the profession, unlike non-educators who might not fully grasp the complexities and offer advice that doesn't resonate (e.g. Why don't you just quit? Just don't do any lesson plans at home!).

Nurturer: Be clear with your teacher friends about the kind of support you need from them. Whether it's just listening or helping find solutions, communicating your needs helps them support you effectively.

Your Thriving Road Map

As we ride with our fellow passengers on this part of our Thriving Journey, remember one of my favorite phrases, "Be the marigold!" It's so easy to get sucked into the drama, negativity, and the walnut pie being served up in the teacher's lounge. Just know that the best thing you can do for your students, your school climate, and your mental well-being is to be the change you want to see in others. Taking time to restore your positive energy by tending to yourself and with other marigolds in your life is the gift you give yourself and others.

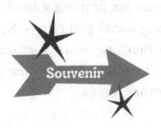

Write down one micro-habit strategy from this chapter that you want to take with you as a souvenir for yourself.

_____

Write down one micro-habit strategy from this chapter that you want to take with you as a souvenir to use at your school or with your students.

_____

Discussion Questions:

1. **Reflecting on Support in Your Professional Environment:** After a school meeting (e.g. team meeting, staff meeting, parent meetings), what emotions do you commonly experience, and how do they reflect the support network or lack thereof within your school? Reflect on the most successful and positive meetings you have had. What elements were present?

2. **Combatting the Negative Energy of "Walnuts":** Considering the concept of emotional contagion, what strategies can you employ to avoid absorbing the negative energy of "walnuts" in your workplace?

3. **Harnessing "Marigold" Energy:** Share a time when the presence of "marigolds" in your professional life made a positive impact on your well-being. How can these experiences inform the way you cultivate and sustain your support network, and what micro-habits can you develop to regularly connect with your marigolds?

4. **The Power of 2 Plus 3:** Reflect on the concept of having two supportive people at work and three outside of work as a formula for burnout prevention. How does this fit into your current support structure, and what intentional steps could you take to strengthen your support network using this concept?

5. **Being the Positive Energy You Wish to See:** How can you actively be the energy in the room during professional gatherings to foster a positive atmosphere? Discuss specific ways you can implement the "Be the Marigold" mindset to be a source of support and inspiration for others, both in staff meetings and in the classroom.

6. **Your Personal Road Map:** Using your Thriving Road Map from Appendix A as a guide, what is one action step you can take immediately to cultivate more work-life alliance? What were your "souvenir" ideas you want to share with students?

Notes

1. Anna Medaris (2023). 6 things researchers want you to know about stress. American Psychological Association. https://www.apa.org/topics/stress/research-findings?utm_source=linkedin&utm_medium=social&utm_campaign=apa-stress&utm_content=sia-research-findings&fbclid=IwAR0Z-NUyeyheS9ej2F7MkCmfAEtJsUPZlILZ0VQIzsoXiZuYIQ66axyG-ys

2. CDC (2023). How Does Social Connectedness Affect Health? Centers for Disease Control and Prevention. https://www.cdc.gov/emotional-wellbeing/social-connectedness/affect-health.htm

3. M. Iacoboni (2008). *Mirroring People*. New York: Picordor.

4. Shawn Achor (2010). *The Happiness Advantage: How a Positive Brain Fuels Success in Work and Life*. New York: Random House.

5. Jennifer Gonzales (2013). Find Your Marigold: The One Essential Rule for New Teachers. *Cult of Pedagogy*. https://www.cultofpedagogy.com/marigolds/

6. Green Cross Academy of Traumatology (n. d.). *Standards of Care*. Green Cross Academy of Traumatology. https://greencross.org/about-gc/standards-of-care-guidelines/

7. Green Cross Academy of Traumatology (n. d.). *Standards of Care*. Green Cross Academy of Traumatology. https://greencross.org/about-gc/standards-of-care-guidelines/

8. Simone Schnall et al. (2008). Social support and the perception of geographical slant. *Journal of Experimental Social Psychology* 44, no. 5, pp. 1246–1255. https://www.sciencedirect.com/science/article/abs/pii/S002210310800070X.

CHAPTER

4

Find Mindful Moments

"I swear, if someone tells me to self-care or join a mindful morning yoga class before or after work one more time, I'm going to scream."

—Jenn, 5th grade teacher

Welcome back! Thus far on our journey, we've made stops to learn about boosting positive energy, cultivating work-life balance, and building support networks. Now, let's take a turn on the path of mindfulness.

Let's start with some reflection. What does the term "mindfulness" mean to you?

Mindfulness is _____.

For some folks, mindfulness is a hippie-dippie woo woo thing that ain't nobody got time for in a busy workday. For others, it is the cornerstone of their well-being. My guess is you fall somewhere in between. For many years, I thought mindfulness was great for my students; for me, my mindful journey stopped at trying yoga and hating how boring it was and downloading the Calm app and forgetting to use it.

Mindfulness, often misconceived as a time-consuming meditation practice, is essentially about being present in the moment without judgment. It's an attention process, focusing on the "now" rather than overthinking the past or worrying about the future. This chapter demystifies mindfulness, showing it's not about hours of sitting meditation, or a silent retreat in the Himalayan mountains wearing a loincloth, but rather about simple, present-moment awareness. I'll also cover the "two-for-one" benefit of mindfulness for you and your students.

Why Mindfulness Is Essential for Burnout Prevention

Chances are, you're aware of the benefits of mindfulness for students. If not, prepare yourself to jump on the mindfulness bus with this data! The research on the benefits of mindfulness for students is more than compelling: it's downright eye-opening. According to a compilation of research from Mindful Schools, teaching mindfulness to students has shown the following benefits for children and teens:[1]

- **Better Attention and Learning Skills** – Mindfulness strengthens self-control, impulse control, focus, attention, cognitive control, and self-discipline.

- **Improved Social, Emotional, and Behavioral Skills** – Mindfulness increases positive moods, improves social skills and peer acceptance, increases confidence; students show better empathy and perspective-taking skills, as well as reduced aggression.

- **More Resilience** – Mindfulness improves emotional regulation, reduces depression and post-traumatic stress symptoms, and lowers anxiety and stress.

But what about the benefits of mindfulness for adults? Yep, it works well for us, too. Research from Shapiro, Schwartz, and Santerre[2] and Galante and her colleagues,[3] among others, shows that adults who practice mindfulness (often meditation practices) show:

- **Increased Happiness and Positive Emotions** – People who meditate actually grow their prefrontal cortex, the part of the brain most responsible for feeling happy.

- **Decreased Stress** – Mindfulness meditation decreases anxiety and negative affect, and lowers emotional reactivity and negative rumination. Meditators show shrinkage of the amygdala, a region of the brain associated with fear, anxiety, and aggression.

- **Better Physical Health** – Mindfulness meditators show increased immune function.

Imagine there was a pill that could grow your brain's left prefrontal cortex, the area responsible for happiness; reduce anxiety, emotional reactivity, and negative rumination by shrinking the amygdala (the fear and aggression center of the brain); and these changes led to increased happiness, decreased stress, and better physical health.

So, let me ask you this: Would you be in line at the CVS pharmacy for this magic pill? I bet you would! Well, the good news is there's no prescription required for these benefits, people! That "pill" is 10 minutes of mindfulness per day. TEN MINUTES.

Look at your screentime data on your phone – how much time is on social media? Swapping out just 10 minutes of that with mindfulness practice could change your well-being trajectory for yourself *and your students.*

Bridging the Research to Your Reality

So why don't we practice mindfulness every day? One reason I think we are not all hook-line-and-sinker practicing mindfulness as self-care every day is a bit more insidious than the "I don't have time" barrier. This reason has to do with your identity as an educator, and your belief that you are the "helper."

You know the saying, "doctors make the worst patients?" This adage can apply to so many professions, including ours. We as educators are incredible at dispensing advice and support about the importance of mindfulness and self-care, and then turn around and NOT do it for ourselves.

We tell a stressed-out teen to practice mindful breathing to reduce stress, and then skip our yoga class or our mindfulness app because we are too busy or too tired. But as the late Chris Peterson, one of the pioneers of positive psychology, once said:

Positive psychology is not a spectator sport.

Oh snap. When I first heard this quote, it hit me like a ton of bricks. I realized that I gotta walk the walk, not just talk the talk. I can't run myself into the ground, never take any downtime, and then expect to be fully present for my students. If I can cultivate being mindful, not "mind-FULL," then not only will I enjoy the benefits, but I will be a more happy, present school psychologist, mom, wife, and friend to others. So really, it's not incongruous to be a helper and take care of myself first. It actually makes me a *better* helper to others.

In this section, I will share the research on mindfulness not just as an abstract concept, but I will also offer up practical strategies for boosting your mindful moments in the school day, starting with yourself. In this way, you can be the "living lesson plan" of mindfulness for your students!

Clearing Your "Emotional Whiteboard"

Mindfulness isn't just a personal or internal process; practicing it has an impact on our interactions, particularly with our students and colleagues. Imagine your principal is having a rough morning. Unbeknownst to you, that morning, she just received news about her aging mother needing hospice care, she got an email from an angry parent, berating her about her latest initiative, and she spilled coffee on her favorite sweater on the way to work that day. You pop in her office to ask about something and she snaps, "Ugh, you need to come back later." You, not knowing anything about the morning she had, start to wonder, "What did I do?" or "Is she mad at me?" or "Did I do something wrong?" And you spend your day partially distracted by the nagging sense something isn't right with your relationship with your principal.

Now, imagine that scenario with your principal practicing mindfulness. She has all the same stressors, but she takes a mindful pause before responding to your request for her time. In this case, when you come in, she takes a breath and expresses her feelings aloud: "I'm sorry I can't meet right now, I have had a stressful morning. I got some bad news and am feeling overwhelmed right now. I can meet this afternoon once I've dealt with this." Even if it's delivered in a less than warm fuzzy tone, chances are, you'll leave this interaction knowing that her mood is not about you, and you can go about your day without the subterrain stress draining your energy in the back of your mind.

As one of my favorite authors, Nataly Kogan writes, every one of us has an invisible "emotional whiteboard" on our chests.[4] Written all over it are our feelings – *whether we say them aloud or not*. Remember from Chapter 3 about humans' uncanny ability to read emotions? If you are feeling stressed, your students pick up on it. Without any explanation, kids naturally wonder if it's something about them that is causing the emotion.

When you express and acknowledge your feelings, you clear your emotional whiteboard for those around you. This transparency helps reduce your stress, models healthy emotional expression for students, and alleviates their anxiety by providing clarity and psychological safety.

Of course, you don't have to go into great personal detail about why you are feeling the way you are. A simple, "Hey class, I had a bad night's sleep and am feeling a little grouchy today" or "I am feeling a little frazzled today because the copier jammed and I didn't get to print off what I hoped to print for you this morning" would suffice. Then, you can model for the class or brainstorm a healthy coping strategy for grouchiness or feeling frazzled.

Adult Recess: A Mindful Break

Imagine you have a student who is dysregulated. Either they have low energy and can't focus on their work, or they're super amped up and distracted from their work. Would you advise this student to stay in from recess every day and continue slogging through work or trying to force focus while they're bouncing off the walls? Or would you give them a break to reboot? Chances are, if you know the research on the benefits of break and movement, you'd send that kid out to recess.

Now, let's flip the script. Do you take breaks or move during the day? Or when the kids are out to recess, do you slog through your inbox or frantically prep the next activity? Research shows that focusing only on your to-do list without breaks can negatively impact your mood and (ironically) kill productivity.[5] On the flip side, brief breaks vastly improve focus.[6]

I'd like to propose the concept of "adult recess" as an invitation to create restorative micro-breaks during your day. Think about your last break; was it rejuvenating? What were you doing? "Adult recess" is about finding what restores you, be it tuning into children's laughter while you're on recess duty, enjoying a cup of tea, or taking a brisk walk around the building. It's about identifying restorative actions that refresh your mind.

Cultivating the Inner Pause Button

The real power of mindfulness lies in the pause it offers between stimulus and response. This pause allows you to label your feelings, take a breath, and choose your actions deliberately. It empowers you to *respond* instead of *react*, transforming how you handle challenging situations. One of the ways you can do this is to visualize the process shown in Figure 4.1.

The next time you are triggered by something – a rude comment from a student, an unfriendly email from a parent, or a request from administration that you don't have time for – choose a mindful pause activity before responding. Some examples include taking a deep breath, counting to 10 in your mind, putting one hand on your heart and the other on your stomach, or reciting a word 3 times like "pause" before you respond.

To cultivate this inner pause button, remind yourself that practicing mindful meditation before school, during breaks, or after school, even for just 10 minutes a day, strengthens your neural connections and rewires your brain to be less reactive. Think of it this way: mindfulness "on the cushion" can strengthen your ability to access mindfulness "off the cushion."

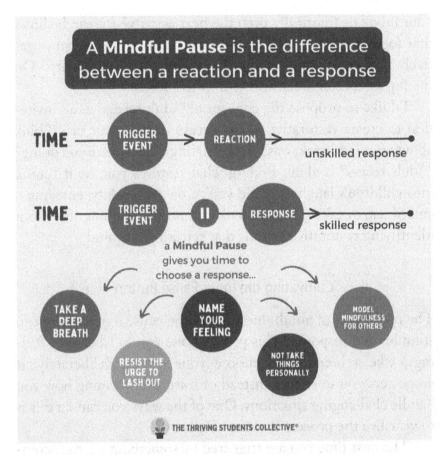

FIGURE 4.1 Benefits of the pause

It's also worth noting that there is a double-down effect of bringing mindfulness into your classroom routines – you and your students strengthen your emotional regulation and impulse control (aka "stop and think" skills). Here's a few suggestions Angela Watson shares in our *How to Reverse Educator Burnout* course:

- Morning Rituals in the Classroom:
  - Create a pleasant morning routine that excites you about the day ahead.

- Engage in activities like turning on decorative lamps, listening to music, and reviewing lesson plans to mentally prepare for teaching.
- Mindfulness Breaks with Students:
  - Observe when students show signs of needing a break (fidgeting, off-task behavior) and respond with a mindfulness break.
  - Incorporate activities like stretching, breathing exercises, guided drawing, or interactive discussions.
- Using Technology Mindfully:
  - Use technology, like GoNoodle, or a mindful app like Headspace for structured mindfulness breaks with students, but avoid relying on devices during your own mindfulness time.

Micro-Habits to Use Your Thrive-O-Gram Strength

Ahhh, it's my favorite section . . . habit hack time! When you think about the compelling research behind mindfulness, why hasn't every human on the planet bought into prioritizing mindful practices? The problem is that mindfulness is simple, but not easy. It's hard to stop and be present, really taking the time to ground yourself and your students to reboot during the busy school day.

The good news is that since our brains love patterns, you can leverage this to build mindfulness in your daily routines. Here are a few ways to take the abstract concept of mindfulness and embed it in your day as an "add in" not an "add on" to your day, based on your Thrive-o-gram strengths profile.

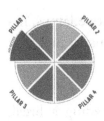

Go-Getter: Challenge yourself to a 30 days of mindfulness routine! Download a guided meditation app and each morning spend 10 minutes meditating to strengthen your inner pause button. Track your streak on the app or in your planner to feel a sense of accomplishment.

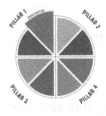

Fascinator: You're going to love learning about mindfulness practices for you and your students! Create a Pinterest board of ideas, make a list of 10 ways to take a pause, research the best mindfulness app, or read some inspirational blog posts about ways to incorporate mindfulness in you and your students' day. Be sure to pair these new ideas with existing routines.

Creator: Hey there visionary! Chances are after reading this chapter you already have some ideas percolating about ways to build mindful moments in your day and into your daily routines with students. Narrow down your ideas to one practice, one time of day, and set the intention to strengthen this connection (e.g. using transitions like the school bell as cues for mindfulness practices, such as taking a deep breath).

Architect: Take some data on how you feel after doing certain activities during "adult recess" (e.g. checking email, taking a walk, looking at social media, doing a guided meditation, interacting with colleagues, etc.). How restorative were the activities, from 1-10? Make strategic adjustments. Do the same process with your students to help them identify what feels restorative for their mood and focus.

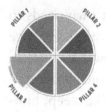

Connector: While you tend to love socializing, don't forget to take quiet moments for yourself during prep time or lunch breaks to decompress. Being with people can be energizing, but also draining at times. Taking time alone can be restorative, too! Resist the urge to check your phone during downtime; instead, use these moments for quiet reflection or deep breathing.

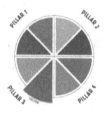

Helper: Your tendency to want to problem solve for others is part of what makes you an amazing helper! You might also look inward to solving your own personal problems during your down time. However, to protect your energy, refrain from checking emails and trying to solve personal problems during school hours to maintain focus and prevent distractions. Instead, utilize short breaks during the day to re-center. This can be as simple as 30 seconds of deep breathing while students are working.

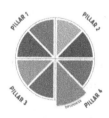

Influencer: You can be the change you want to see in others! By embodying mindfulness practices, you are influencing your colleagues and students while also recharging your own energy. Whenever you feel like you don't have time for mindfulness, remind yourself "I can be the living lesson plan for my students." During breaks, focus on clearing your head and reconnecting with your purpose. Model for your students through routines like morning mindfulness, mid-day stretch breaks, or afternoon "zen time."

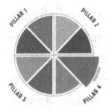

Nurturer: Pay attention to your own needs to prevent overwhelm and exhaustion. Practice curiosity and compassion toward yourself, especially when feeling emotionally deregulated. Identify unmet needs, like sleep, hunger, or the need for a break.

Your Thriving Road Map

Don't forget to take exits from your busy day down Mindfulness Road on your Thriving Journey. By cultivating your inner pause button, you can regulate your own stress and serve as a model for your students to reap the benefits of mindfulness.

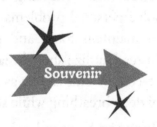

Write down one micro-habit strategy from this chapter that you want to take with you as a souvenir for yourself.

_____

Write down one micro-habit strategy from this chapter that you want to take with you as a souvenir to use at your school or with your students.

_____

Discussion Questions:

1. **Personal Definitions of Mindfulness:** How do you define mindfulness in the context of your own life and teaching practice? How does this definition reflect in your daily interactions with students and colleagues? What micro-habits can you use to be truly present and model mindfulness for your students?

2. **Mindfulness Misconceptions:** How can educators address common misconceptions about mindfulness to better integrate mindful practices into their busy schedules? Discuss one way you can plan a small, practical step toward incorporating mindfulness into daily life.

3. **Mindfulness and Identity as Educators:** Considering the quote "Positive psychology is not a spectator sport," reflect on how the identity of being a "helper" might interfere with personal self-care practices. How can educators reconcile the need to support others with the necessity of mindfulness for their own well-being?

4. **The Inner Pause Button:** In moments of stress or frustration, how can the practice of hitting your "inner pause button" change the outcome of interactions with students or colleagues? Share a time when a mindful pause could have or did benefit a challenging situation.

5. **Micro-Habits for Mindful Practices:** What small, achievable micro-habits could you introduce to your routine to create mindful moments throughout the school day? Discuss the idea of "Adult Recess" and how short breaks could be implemented for personal mindfulness practice as well as for fostering mindfulness among students.

6. **Your Personal Road Map:** Using your Thriving Road Map from Appendix A as a guide, what is one action step you can take immediately to cultivate more work-life alliance? What were your "souvenir" ideas you want to share with students?

Notes

1. Mindful Schools (n.d.). Research on Mindfulness and Education. Mindful Schools. https://www.mindfulschools.org/about-mindfulness/research-on-mindfulness/
2. S. L. Shapiro, G. E. R., Schwartz, and C. Santerre (2005). Meditation and Positive Psychology. In C. R. Snyder, & S. J. Lopez (Eds.), *Handbook of Positive Psychology*. Cary, NC: Oxford University Press. https://scirp.org/reference/referencespapers?referenceid=1343210
3. Julieta Galante et al. (2023). Systematic review and individual participant data meta-analysis of randomized controlled trials assessing mindfulness-based programs for mental health promotion. *NATURE MENTAL HEALTH*. https://www.nature.com/articles/s44220-023-00081-5
4. Nataly Kogan (2022). *The Awesome Human Project: Break Free from Daily Burnout, Struggle Less, and Thrive More in Work and Life*. Louisville, CO: Sounds True, Inc.
5. Patricia Albulescu et al. (2022). "Give me a break!" A systematic review and meta-analysis on the efficacy of micro-breaks for increasing well-being and performance. PLoS One. https://www.ncbi.nlm.nih.gov/pmc/articles/PMC9432722/
6. University of Illinois at Urbana-Champaign (2011). Brief diversions vastly improve focus, researchers find. *Science Daily*. https://www.sciencedaily.com/releases/2011/02/110208131529.htm

CHAPTER

5

Reduce Frustration

"I feel like I am treading water and just trying to make it through each day. I'm frustrated with the lack of support in our district and lack of personnel to help."

—Kendra, high school teacher

In this journey to Thrive Town, we've explored our strengths, aligned with our values, built support networks, and integrated mindfulness into our daily routine. Now, let's dive into a crucial systems-level topic: reducing frustration, or as I call it in our *Reverse Educator Burnout* course, being stuck in the "bureaucracy traffic jam."

Let's start with a reflection.

What is your greatest work struggle right now? _____

No matter what stressor you wrote down, chances are, there's an element about it that is out of your hands. Our schools have systemic challenges – overcrowded classrooms, a shortage of mental health support providers, lack of support for neurodivergent students, systemic racism, underfunded mandates to serve special education students, students living in poverty coming to school without basic needs being met, and the list goes on. It's easy to get frustrated by it all. So here you are, stuck in traffic, wanting to get to Thrive Town, but instead, you just shake your fist at the injustice of the slow pace of getting kids what they need for you to do your job well.

One crucial lesson in my journey as a school psychologist is how to address the frustration with problem-solving and how to let go of picking a fight with reality. When we resist what currently *is*, we add more stress to our already heavy load. For instance, facing a high caseload and a shortage of school psychologists, while knowing no new hires are on the horizon, is undoubtedly stressful. But constantly ruminating over the unfairness only amplifies our distress.

To combat frustration, we can turn to acceptance. Acceptance doesn't mean liking the situation; it means acknowledging the reality without fighting it. This acceptance serves as our starting point for problem-solving.

Why Reducing Frustration Is Essential for Burnout Prevention

I remember working in a school that had a policy to send out forms three times to parents in the mail before emailing them the form. *Buy why?* No one could provide a reason. It was a policy that likely came out of a knee-jerk reaction to one time when emailing went awry. But with my caseload of 75 students, it was a real pain. With every single form I put in ye olde pony express snail mail, I seethed in anger at the stupidity of it all. That in turn, put me in a bad mood, *nearly every day*. I asked every individual "why?!?" and asked anyone who would listen. No one had an answer, which only made me more frustrated.

Finally, my supervisor told me something that alleviated my frustration: "In bureaucracies, you must free yourself from the frustration of 'why,' just focus on the good, and change what you can control." My colleagues and I banded together and emailed the director of special education about the issue, offered up a solution to email first and then mail the forms if there was no response. And until it was addressed, I stopped picking a fight with reality. When I had to mail the forms, I recited "free yourself from why!" I also reframed to find the good, by thinking to myself, "Mailing this form is helpful for parents who do not have access to consistent internet." And most importantly, I no longer whipped myself up into an annoyed frenzy that would ruin my mood and my day.

You might be thinking, "But isn't that resigning yourself to the dysfunction?" If we all resign ourselves to a broken system and dumb policies, nothing will change! Shouldn't we be trying to change the dysfunctional system from within? Absolutely! But the key is to pick your battles and accept the reality that some battles, when taken on alone, will drain your life force and are therefore losing ones. This next section will teach you how to know the difference.

Bridging the Research to Your Reality

Here's a bonkers statistic for you, from a leading researcher in wellness, Sonja Lyubomirsky. Only 10% of our total happiness comes from external circumstances![1] This is probably why changing districts three times didn't really change my level of burnout. The grass wasn't greener in the other district; it was a different kind of grass, with different stressors. In one district, I struggled with volume of cases I was assigned. In another, I had low volume of cases but high complexity. In a third, my student caseload was great, but the parent pressure on me was intense and litigious. So, wherever I went, there I was, with my walnut-y mindset following me. It wasn't until I shifted my mindset and habits that I was able to bloom in whatever district I was planted in.

No doubt there are real stressors in your current role. That is a reality! I'm definitely not suggesting that it's all in your head. This chapter is an invitation to follow the research, which suggests that whether or not you are able to find happiness at work depends quite a bit on how you view your circumstances. There's a different type of bureaucracy traffic jam that leads to frustration in every district, but it's how you respond to the frustration that makes a difference in your well-being. Let's dig in on a few practical strategies to do this!

The Power of Naming

When we experience frustrating situations, we may not even recognize the underlying emotion we are experiencing. Frustration comes in different flavors. A less strong version of frustration is irritation, and a stronger version is anger or rage. When we experience these emotions, our amygdala detects a threat, and our options default to fight or flight, neither of which works well in a school setting—what am I going to do, challenge my special education director to a fight? Flee in the middle of a stressful staff meeting? Fortunately, there's another way to tame frustration!

Research shows that simply naming our stress can significantly diminish the power of negative emotions in our brain, particularly the amygdala, which is responsible for our fight or flight response.[2] By acknowledging feelings like "I'm frustrated," "I'm irritated," or "I'm tired," we can reduce the intensity of the amygdala's response, bringing a sense of calm. An easy way to remember this research is by the phrase from Dr. Dan Siegel, "Name it to tame it!"

It's also important to practice using specific language that is proportional to the situation. Emotions have granularity; there's a difference between irritation and rage, though they are both related to anger. Try to name your emotions proportional to the scale of the issue.

Another strategy is to replace knee-jerk extreme words you tend to use in your self-talk with less dramatic terms. For instance, instead of saying "I am so pissed off I have dismissal duty," try "I dislike dismissal duty, but I can manage it." Try replacing words like "impossible" and "unbearable" with words like "challenging" or "difficult" and see how it changes how you feel.

Conducting a Control Audit

When overwhelmed, our brains tend to get stuck in a loop of stress and frustration. By conducting a "control audit," we move our focus to the prefrontal cortex, the area responsible for thinking and reasoning. This shift allows us to transition from a state of being overwhelmed to actionable steps. We start by acknowledging our feelings, then list out factors we can't control and those we can. Then, we can take one thing from our "things we can control" list and start there. This exercise helps us focus on what we *can* influence, giving us a sense of control amid chaos.

I like to use the following mental sequence when I am stuck in frustration: Allow, accept, decide. This is a real example, by the way!

1. Allow: First, I allow my feelings to be there. My feelings are there to tell me something. I name my feelings. (e.g. I feel underappreciated and frustrated because I do not have a private space to work with children and I have to test in a dark janitor's closet with no window).

2. Accept: Next, I accept that this is what is happening for now. I don't have to love what's going on or resign myself that it will always be this way to accept it (e.g. This is the current reality. I have to work in a "cloffice" – closet/office).

3. Decide: Finally, I decide what is in my hands. (e.g. I can't create a new space in a building, but I can express to the principal and my supervisor that we need a creative solution so I can do my job).

What situations create frustration for you? Can you practice acceptance instead of picking a fight with the current reality, which adds stress on top of stress? Remember, acceptance doesn't mean you like it or are resigned to it, only that you see the reality in front of you and can make a choice about how to respond.

It's worth noting that there are some heavy realities – racism, sexism, homophobia, and prejudice in our society – that compound educator stress to a whole new level, especially for those educators in historically marginalized groups. These big issues can feel overwhelming to tackle on our own with just our mindsets. This is where the power of the community comes into play.

In terms of deciding what you can influence, you may or may not be in a position of privilege to advocate for change vocally. Other avenues include finding your marigolds and allies in your school you can band together with or joining an affinity group. For example, some educators find it helpful to find a support group to voice frustrations in a safe space and feel heard by others going through similar challenges. And if you do have a position of leadership, authority, or privilege, I encourage you to speak up in staff meetings to support colleagues advocating for change. Call out microaggressions and other injustices, stand with those pushing for better working conditions and educational practices, and initiate or join efforts to improve the school environment constructively.

Reframing Stress

Our implicit beliefs, or mindsets, about stress greatly influence how we experience it. If we believe stress is bad, our brain will seek evidence to confirm this belief, often overlooking moments of appreciation or support. Stress is our body's response to a situation that requires attention or action, so we do need the stress response. Chronic stress without coping is when stress can start to take a toll. By shifting our mindset and viewing stress as an opportunity for growth and learning, we can decrease its negative effects.[3]

This mindset shift is called "reframing." Reframing our stress as something insightful can profoundly change our perspective. Reframing, sometimes called "cognitive restructuring," has been shown to reduce fear, anxiety, and other negative emotions in the short and long term.[4] With that in mind, here are a few "reframes" about stress you might want to try on for size:

- **Stress means we care.** We often stress about things we care about deeply. For example, my concern over high caseloads and underfunding in schools stems from a deep passion for children's mental health. Understanding that our stress can signify our passions helps us find meaning in our struggles.

- **Stress is insightful.** Acknowledge your feelings, but don't let them control you. Think about stress as a guide, pointing you to areas needing change. Stressed about how to support your neurodivergent students in your class? Take that cue as an opportunity to level up your learning or seek consultation for a hard-to-reach student.

- **Stress helps us grow.** When managed effectively, stress can serve as a catalyst for personal growth and peak performance. Stress can also help you build resilience, which is important for emotional health. For example, after facing a difficult parent meeting, you might feel more equipped to handle it in the future.

We'll cover this more in Chapter 8, "Reduce Daily Stress," but it's worth mentioning here in the context of frustration, since that is a common emotion when we hit the bureaucracy traffic jam.

Reframe Mundane as Meaningful

Research shows that when you find meaning in your tasks, you are 2-3 times more likely to complete them, make fewer mistakes, and feel good about completing them.[5]

As educators, we often have paperwork tasks that don't feel as meaningful as student interactions. And when you are frustrated because you must do a drudgery task, it's easy to get sucked into frustration and negative thinking.

For me, as a school psychologist, the task that could get me stuck at a frustration station on my road to Thrive Town is writing reports. If you don't know, school psychologists assess students one-on-one (fun!) and then have to write up a lengthy legally complex report about it that virtually no one reads in its entirety (not fun!). So many days I've sat in front of my laptop, grumbling at how I have to write these boring reports. But what if I viewed it differently? Instead of thinking, "I'm writing up these boring reports" I can reframe to, "I am writing a report to help a child understand how they learn best and give the support team a better understanding of their learning profile for interventions." Suddenly, my motivation is rekindled because there is meaning behind my task.

What routine tasks can you reframe? Grading papers can be reframed as opportunities to understand your students' learning progress and prepare better for the future. Cutting out paper is preparing engaging learning opportunities for students. Tracking data is a way to clearly track student progress and show success. Suddenly, a tedious task becomes more tolerable because there's a reason behind it that is important to you.

Micro-Habits to Use Your Thrive-O-Gram Strength

How can we habit-hack coping with frustration? What are small steps you can take when you are fed up with the system, policies, or anything that feels overwhelming or out of your hands? Let's talk about the science behind learned helplessness vs. learned optimism.

Learned helplessness is a behavioral phenomenon in which you believe you have no control over a situation. It is the result of repeated exposure to stressors and adverse events. When we're overcome by learned helplessness, we typically display a pessimistic explanatory style, meaning we view adverse events as being internal (e.g. "I can't handle all these kids with learning and behavioral problems in my class") and unalterable (e.g. "I'm never going to get the help I need from my administration"). You can see why these beliefs would not empower you to take action.

Learned optimism, on the other hand, is a concept that says we can change our behaviors by recognizing and challenging our negative self-talk.[6] We view our situation as changeable, through internal work (e.g. "I can take a course on how to help kids with ADHD in the classroom"). We also view adverse events as temporary and changeable (e.g. "Right now I don't have any extra support, but I can work with admin to find a path to more support."). This process of allowing the thought, then reframing the pessimistic thoughts to develop more positive behaviors, can be cultivated.

Here's a fun study about that. When people are optimistic, they see more opportunities. In one crazy example, pessimists were less likely to see a man in a gorilla suit run across a basketball court than optimists![7] When we are frustrated, our vision literally narrows. When we allow the frustration and then reframe pessimistic thoughts, our vision opens, and we can start to see possibility. It doesn't remove the stressor, but it gives you a path for change.

Remember what you wrote about what is your greatest frustration? Let's reframe it!

_____ is frustrating, and this means _____
(insert positive thought, like I care, I can learn, I will grow)
_____ is frustrating right now, but I can _____
(insert positive action step)

Want to learn more tips to manage your frustration? Check out the following suggestions, based on your Thrive-o-gram strengths profile. Grab your favorite souvenirs on the trip to Thrive Town – one for you and one for your students. They can also benefit from strategies to boost their ability to manage frustration as well, and you can be the catalyst!

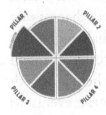 **Go-Getter:** Since you love to-do lists, get out a piece of paper and list all the ideas you can think of to tackle your most frustrating situation. Think outside the practical box and write freely. Then, circle the idea you want to try

this week and put it on your calendar. Remember that one of your burnout traps is trying to do everything, so give yourself grace and pick *one thing* that would make a difference.

Fascinator: Hope is one of your core strengths, which translates nicely into the idea of reframing frustration thoughts into action! When you catch yourself in a negative thought, try the "2-for-1" technique. For each negative thought, think of two positive thoughts (e.g. "I'm frustrated because my school doesn't have enough resources for our struggling readers" can turn into "I care about my students' reading skills" and "I can research low- or no-cost supports with my Multi-Tiered Systems of Support team members."

Creator: One of your burnout traps is when others do not see your creative vision for improvement and hop on board with your ideas right away. You can see ways to achieve positive change before most, so meet people where they are. Acknowledge frustration (yours and others!), allow the feeling, and then do a control audit. Who is with me? Can I form a coalition of the willing first instead of fighting the reality that change is harder for some people than others?

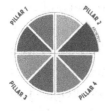

Architect: With your strategic thinking strength, reducing frustration by taking action is an area where you can really shine! For example, if you are frustrated because the school's reading curriculum isn't working for a particular student, instead of just troubleshooting your frustration with that one student's progress, you can zoom out to class-wide or school-wide level interventions. Join a leadership team, set up a time to meet with an interventionist in your school, listen in on the next district-wide curriculum meeting, find research-based intervention alternatives yourself, and share your ideas with your grade level or leadership teams.

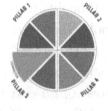 **Connector:** With collaboration as one of your strengths, banding together with others who share similar frustration about systemic problems is a path to collective positive action. At staff meetings, or at lunchtime chats, listen to how others around you process frustration. Do they refrain from just venting every day? Do they reframe challenging situations with positivity? Or do they have good ideas for change? Band together with those people! Agree with them out loud and publicly so they feel supported in their good ideas. Find time to connect and collaborate, either formally on a committee, or informally over lunch or in a weekly after school brainstorming session.

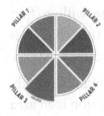 **Helper:** Since you love to help, one of your biggest burnout traps is when helping someone is out of your hands. Despite best efforts, there are some systemic forces that are beyond your control, and this is a source of frustration. Here's a jedi mind trick for that: Have you heard of the term "radical acceptance?" This is a practice where you accept the challenges you face without necessarily loving them. Radical

acceptance involves focusing on changing what you can and reframing your stress to take action on controllable aspects. Your mantra could be, "I don't have to do the whole world, I just have to do me the best I can."

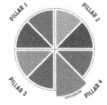

Influencer: With your natural positivity, charisma, and leadership, it's likely you are already involved in a few initiatives for systemic change! It's important for you to be self-aware if you're suppressing your own feelings of frustration instead of allowing them to be present. Due to your natural enthusiasm, you may tend to overlook potential challenges and setbacks. It's important to balance your positivity with a realistic perspective, acknowledging potential obstacles and preparing for them. This can help you navigate difficult situations more effectively and create more sustainable success for your students and colleagues.

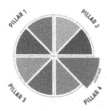

Nurturer: Self-compassion is one of your core strengths, which comes in very handy when facing frustration! The key is to prioritize yourself when you're feeling overwhelmed, which can be difficult since you tend to prioritize others' well-being. In frustrating moments, ask yourself, "What advice would I give a best friend if they were in this situation?" and then take your own advice.

Your Thriving Road Map

In conclusion, while reframing stress and conducting control audits may not eliminate systemic barriers causing chronic stress, they can significantly reduce its impact. Remember, it's not about fixing everything at once; it's about doing your best each day!

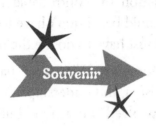

Write down one micro-habit strategy from this chapter that you want to take with you as a souvenir for yourself.

_____

Write down one micro-habit strategy from this chapter that you want to take with you as a souvenir to use at your school or with your students.

_____

Discussion Questions:

1. **Reflecting on Systemic Challenges:** What are some systemic issues that contribute to your daily frustrations, and how do you typically react to them? Reflect on your past reactions to a frustrating event and identify one way you could have handled things differently to cope with these challenges.

2. **The Role of Acceptance in Problem-Solving:** How can acceptance of things we cannot change lead to more effective problem-solving for the challenges we do have control over? Discuss ways in which you can help differentiate between accepting reality and resigning to dysfunction.

3. **Naming and Reframing Frustrations:** What are some frustrations you've recently experienced, and how can the practice of naming them help in reducing their impact? How can you extend the "Name It to Tame it" philosophy with your students?

4. **Conducting a Control Audit:** Reflect on a current frustration and conduct a control audit. What aspects are within your control, and what action steps can you take?

5. **The Power of 2-for-1 Reframing:** Think of a recent work-related frustration and apply the 2-for-1 reframing technique: for each negative thought, identify two positive ones. How does this practice alter your perception of the situation?

6. **Your Personal Road Map:** Using your Thriving Road Map from Appendix A as a guide, what is one action step you can take immediately to cultivate more work-life alliance? What were your "souvenir" ideas you want to share with students?

Notes

1. S. Luinomirsky, K. Sheldon, and D. Schade (2005) Pursuing happiness: The architecture of sustainable change. *Review of General Psychology*, 9, 111–31.

2. Matthew D. Lieberman et al. (2007). Putting Feelings into Words: Affect Labeling Disrupts Amygdala Activity in Response to Affective Stimuli. *Psychological Science*. https://pubmed.ncbi.nlm.nih.gov/17576282/

3. Clifton B. Parker (2015). Embracing stress is more important than reducing stress, Stanford psychologist says. *Stanford News*. https://news.stanford.edu/2015/05/07/stress-embrace-mcgonigal-050715/

4. Ashley A Shurick et al. (2012). Durable effects of cognitive restructuring on conditioned fear. https://pubmed.ncbi.nlm.nih.gov/22775125/

5. Shawn Achor (2011). Make Stress Work for You. *Harvard Business Review*. https://hbr.org/2011/02/make-stress-work-for-you

6. Martin Seligman (1998). *Learned Optimism: How to Change Your Mind and Your Life*. New York: Free Press.

7. D. J. Simons and C. F. Chabris (1999). Gorillas in our midst: Sustained inattentional blindness for dynamic events. *Perception* 28, 1059–1074.

CHAPTER

6

Protecting Your Downtime

"I feel like I just sprint with all my energy to winter break, collapse, sprint to spring break, collapse, and then do a final sprint to summer break, and collapse."

—Michael, school psychologist

Welcome back to our Thrive Town journey, where we are more than halfway through our exploration of educator well-being! In this chapter, we focus on a crucial aspect of thriving: protecting your downtime.

Let's start with a reflection.

When do you rest? _____

When I do this activity with educators in professional development or during keynote sessions, rarely does anyone say, "during the school day" or "every night and weekend." It's usually "when I finally get to sleep" or "on summer break."

Why do educators struggle with resting and protecting their downtime, despite knowing its importance? It's because of a big ol' mindset prison we put ourselves in every day: "I'll rest when I'm done with X, Y, or Z." However, in the world of education, work is never truly done. I often say, "Kids are never done, so we will never be done." If we wait until we're finished to rest, we'll never get the chance. Once we've accepted that truth, the next step is finding effective rest strategies throughout your day and reframing rest as an activity that is productive in itself.

Let's dive into why rest is not just important, but *essential* for your well-being and productivity.

Why Protecting Your Downtime Is Essential for Burnout Prevention

Rest is not just a break from productivity; it's a catalyst for it. Here's what the research shows are some key benefits of rest:[1]

- **Boosts Productivity:** Resting parts of our brain that need it makes us more efficient when we return to work.

- **Improves Mood:** We are more efficient and creative when in a good mood, which rest can facilitate.

- **Enhances Creativity:** The default mode network in our brain, responsible for integrating information, is activated during rest, leading to more "aha" moments.

- **Physical and Mental Health:** Rest, particularly combined with movement, can improve our physical and mental well-being.

Extensive work requires proportionate recovery. Here's a metaphor to remember this: Just as Olympic athletes require rest days, educators need downtime to avoid "mental injuries" that lead to burnout. Here's another way of thinking about it in relation to your journey to Thrive Town: Ignoring the signs of depletion is akin to ignoring a car's check engine light – it only leads to more extensive recovery efforts later.

Bridging the Research to Your Reality

Ironically, yesterday, I was muscling through this section, trying to work out the perfect transition between these sections, and getting nowhere. I kept at it far too long, racking my tired brain for the words, and nothing felt right. Then, I decided to take my own advice, and let it rest. I took the dogs for a walk, baked with my daughters, and did mostly nothing. I got a good night's sleep, returned to it today, and voilà, this transition paragraph just came out with ease! Let's explore why that is.

Default Mode Network

Ever wonder why you suddenly have insights in the shower? Or you wake up after a good night's sleep with a brand-new idea on how to solve a problem you've been puzzling on the day before? That's because of the Default Mode Network (DMN). The DMN is a unique cluster of neurons in the brain that becomes active when we are not focusing on the outside world and the brain is at rest. It plays a vital role in processing and integrating information gathered throughout the day.

When we rest, the DMN kicks in. This network is responsible for a range of internal mental activities, including daydreaming, envisioning the future, recalling memories, and considering others' perspectives. By allowing the brain to wander and reflect, the DMN contributes significantly to creative thinking and problem-solving. It's during these periods of rest that we often experience those "aha" moments – sudden insights or realizations that seem to come out of nowhere. I have heard the DMN called the "Do Mostly Nothing" part of our brains, and that's the vibe you're going for!

Unfortunately, our modern lifestyles often don't allow sufficient downtime for the DMN to engage fully. Constant stimulation from technology and the pressure to be always "on" can impede the DMN's natural process. This is why consciously protecting downtime and allowing for periods of rest, without external distractions, is crucial for mental well-being and creativity. Here are a few practical ways to harness the creative power of the DMN.

- **Schedule Downtime:** Actively set aside time for activities that allow your mind to wander, such as daydreaming, meditating, or taking a leisurely walk. Be careful with watching TV as a "downtime" activity, especially if it's an activating show. There's a difference between 20 minutes of a funny show and hours watching the news. Ideally, TV time is a separate relaxation activity, as it is often stimulating.

- **Reduce Constant Stimulation:** Take breaks from screens and technology to give your DMN the chance to activate. On the way home, turn off all extra stimulation, like music or a podcast and drive in silence. On this "Thrive Drive" your brain will have a chance to fully process the day's events.

- **Mindfulness and Meditation:** Practices like mindfulness and meditation can encourage brain states that activate the DMN.

By understanding and valuing the role of the Default Mode Network, we can harness the power of rest to enhance creativity, problem-solving abilities, and overall mental well-being. Taking time to "do mostly nothing" aligns perfectly with the philosophy that rest is not just a break from productivity, but a vital component of it.

Sleep

If there were one intervention to promote rest that would boost mood, focus, productivity, and well-being it would probably be sleep. Sleep deprivation, even just getting one less hour per day of the recommended eight hours, has the same cognitive effect of being over the legal limit for alcohol consumption (and similarly, people report they are fine when they are actually impaired). Increasing your sleep to the recommended level has been shown to prevent depression, anxiety, and ADHD-like symptoms.[2]

That research, among others, has demonstrated a strong link between better sleep and emotional health. In healthy individuals, good-quality sleep is linked with a more positive mood – and it takes just one night of sleep deprivation to trigger a robust spike in anxiety and depression the following morning! Piggybacking on the last chapter, where we learned the importance of reframing negative events, it's noteworthy that people who suffer from chronic sleep disruption tend to experience daily events as more negative. When we lose sleep, we lose positivity, and all the delightful cognitive and emotional benefits of happiness we learned in Chapter 1.[3]

Chances are, you don't need a lot of convincing about the power of sleep, but a few micro-habits to make a move in the positive direction about getting more zzz's. Here are a few sleep hygiene strategies:

- Maintain a regular sleep schedule: Go to bed and wake up at the same time every day, even on weekends. Start with a fail-safe micro-habit like going to bed five minutes earlier than usual.

- Create a bedtime routine: Engage in calming activities before bed, like reading or taking a warm bath.

- Optimize your sleep environment: Ensure your bedroom is dark, quiet, and cool.

- Invest in a comfortable mattress and pillows: Make sure your bedding is supportive and comfortable.

- Limit exposure to screens: Turn off electronic devices at least an hour before bedtime to reduce blue light exposure. Set a recurring alarm on your phone with a 30 minute warning that it's almost time to shut down.

- Put your phone out of reach: Need help with resisting late night scrolling? Try the strategy sleep advocate Arianna Huffington uses to reduce phone temptation: Put your phone to "bed" in a different room. She literally has an adorable little bed that she tucks her phone into to charge for the night! If you use your phone for an alarm, just kick it old school and get an alarm clock for waking.

- Exercise regularly: Regular physical activity can help you fall asleep faster and enjoy deeper sleep.

- Watch your diet: Avoid heavy meals, caffeine, and alcohol close to bedtime.

- Manage stress: Practice relaxation techniques like meditation or deep breathing to manage stress levels.

- Limit naps: If you must nap, keep it short – about 20 to 30 minutes –and earlier in the afternoon.

- Get some sunlight: Exposure to natural light during the day helps to regulate your sleep-wake cycle.

Water

This strategy falls under, "Yeah, I know, I know!" and yet, we tend not to do it. Hydration is key for focus. Research shows that staying hydrated can lead to an increase in productivity by as much as 14%.[4] Get one of those giant water bottles that break down drinking in smaller time chunks so you can hydrate throughout the day. Added benefit is you get a movement break when you have to use the restroom!

Movement Breaks

Incorporate movement breaks into your day. These can be simple activities like stretching, a quick walk, or even just standing up from your desk. It doesn't have to be rigorous movement either. Just walking for 20 minutes a day has been shown to reduce symptoms of depression.[5]

Do movement breaks with your students for a double benefit! Find a fun movement video, do a mindful movement break app together, or even play a song and have a dance break with your students if that's your thing.

Nature Breaks and Biophilic Design

Being in nature has been shown to have restorative properties. Nature is slow. Nature doesn't judge, it just is what it is. Fresh air is invigorating. Looking at beauty and being in awe of nature is healing. If you have the means to get outside and be in nature, even if it's just briefly marveling at the clouds in the sky or noticing and being in awe of a determined ant carrying away a Cheeto 100x its body weight on the recess yard, little nature breaks can be restorative.

Reality check. Some schools are in places where nature is not abundant, weather doesn't permit a lot of outside time, or safety is an issue. Or you may not have enough time on your breaks to get outside. There's an alternative! If you can't access nature directly, bring nature to you. Biophilic design, the concept of incorporating natural elements into your environment, can reduce stress and boost mood. Simple ways to do this include playing nature sounds, using nature screen savers, or having plants in your workspace. Even the color green has been shown to have a calming effect.[6] For inspiration on a biophilic makeover in your classroom or office, come down a Pinterest rabbit hole with me and check out my Biophilic Design Pinterest board @ thrivingschoolpsych!

Micro-Habits to Use Your Thrive-O-Gram Strength

Take a moment to reflect on how you can integrate rest into your routine. Could it be a specific time set aside for a break? Or maybe a small change in your environment to encourage relaxation? What is your metaphorical "rest stop" on your way to Thrive Town? Remember what you wrote about when you rest (at the start of this chapter)? Let's change it to incorporate your favorite strategy for rest during the day!

When do you rest? _____

Now, let's turn to another important habit to cultivate: protecting your downtime after work. This habit is one that seems so easy in theory but is hard to do in practice. Why is that? For one thing, our brains are more of a "dial" than a "switch." We can't just walk through our front door at home and immediately switch to relaxing. We need time to dial down our work brain and dial up our relaxing brain. Here's one of my favorite habit hacks for this: post-work detox rituals.

Step 1: Reframe Moments of Choice

In those moments when you're debating whether to continue working or to rest, remind yourself that a rested mind is more productive. This conscious choice can help you prioritize rest and give you mental permission to leave a stack of work at work, even though it is unfinished.

Step 2: Pick a Ritual

Create routines to transition from work mode to downtime. This could be a walk with your dog, where a specific landmark on your walk, like a bridge, signifies shifting your focus from work to relaxation. Maybe you change into relaxing clothes and light a candle and do a 10-minute meditation on an app. Perhaps it's doing something incompatible with thinking about work, like reading a book. Moving your body is an excellent way to destress and shift the mood, so maybe you pick a favorite song to listen to or have a private "I'm finished with work" dance party.

As I speak across the country to educators and child service providers, I collect cool shut-down rituals, and here are a few more that incorporate visualization that I love:

- One teacher told me that she hangs her school lanyard on her rearview mirror and tells herself, "The day is behind me."
- Another teacher shared that she imagines her day as a book, and she mentally closes it at the end of the day.

- A school psychologist shared that before she gets out of her car and walks into her home, she eats a piece of chocolate, taking time to savor it as it melts, as the day melts away.

My ritual? I lower my standing desk, and turn off my computer (not just close it) and recite, "I am shutting down. I did my best, and I let go of the rest." Whatever the activity, the key is to find something that works for you to dial down your brain from high-energy work mode to a more relaxed state. (And if you have a cool ritual, share with me on social media @thrivingschoolpsych; I'd love to hear it!)

Step 3: Repeat with Low Friction

Another key to make sure this new shut down ritual habit sticks is that it is repeatable and easy to do. The habit must be a "low friction" task, meaning there aren't many steps to it, and it is easy to do on a daily basis. For example, if you say your post-work detox ritual is to go to the gym, that is a great goal, but it's also full of steps – join a gym, pack your workout clothes, drive to a gym, find parking, change, and finally, workout. That high level of friction will likely keep you from sustaining that habit over time. Pick a lower friction ritual that is easy to do, and then on higher energy days, you can do the higher friction one.

Friction usually takes one of three forms: time, distance, or effort. Removing or reducing any of those three things will increase your chances of success. For example, one study showed that people who lived 5.1 miles from the gym went only once a month, but those who lived within 3.7 miles went five times a month or more.[7]

Want to learn more tips to rest more both inside and outside of work? Check out the following suggestions, based on your Thrive-o-gram strengths profile. Grab your favorite souvenirs on the trip to Thrive Town – one for you and one for your students. Building in rest and restorative breaks will benefit them, too!

Go-Getter: I know, I know, you thrive when you crush your to-do list. I won't ask you to give up your beloved planner and Post-its! But let's give your to-do lists and calendar a "hug." What I mean by that is we tend to pack our days for productivity but rarely build in buffer time. Say you need to plan a parent meeting. Give that parent meeting a restful "hug" around it. Put five minutes of rest before and after the scheduled parent meeting. Also, schedule longer rest periods on your calendar as if they were to-do items (e.g. Pop on your calendar 10 minutes of restorative silence, a calming playlist, or doing deep breathing with a mindfulness app during the day when kids are at recess).

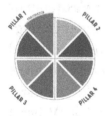

Fascinator: Knowing what is "enough" to give each day is hard, especially for a Fascinator, who has a deep thirst for knowledge. Your new challenge is to accept that there is always something more you could be doing for a student that would help them, but that doesn't mean you have to act on it. If you only have 70% energy today, and you give 70% to your students, that's technically 100% of what you have to give. Don't push yourself past your limits! When you find yourself saying, "I could do more" remind yourself: "I can do more when I am rested."

Creator: Want to tap into your well of creativity? There's no better way than through rest (remember the Default Mode Network research?). Lack of rest slows down your thinking, and coming up with solutions to problems when you have nothing left to give is harder.

This means that rest should be one of the highest priorities on your list! Find a post-work detox ritual and set aside substantial swaths of downtime on the weekend for your creative mind to restore.

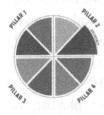

Architect: One of your strengths is to take a "satellite view" of problems, so let's do that for yourself! Take some time to think about your day and how much rest you build into it. Is there anything that is a drain on your energy that you are doing, that you think you "should" be doing, that you can let go of? Are there routines you can build into your classroom or workflow? How much sleep are you getting? Exercise? Water? Track data for a week and see if you can detect any patterns and make adjustments (e.g. "I notice when I drink water in the day, I feel more energetic," or "When I said no to the extra PTA event and yes to my rest, I felt restored the next day").

Connector: Developing new habits can be challenging, so enlist a buddy! Whether it's leaving work at a certain time or taking walking breaks together, having someone to share these goals with can make them more achievable. Do a 10K step challenge with a friend, text each other encouraging messages/check-ins, or sign up for a class with a friend so they can help keep you accountable to show up!

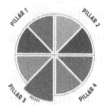

Helper: Just because you love to help people doesn't mean you don't have limits on what you can give. Tune into your own energy levels to calibrate how much you have left to give. As a helper, you need to overflow with energy so you can give without depletion. One cue that you need to prioritize rest is feeling resentful. When you start to feel resentment, it's usually a sign a boundary needs to be set. For example, you might offer to help a friend move on the weekend, but then you feel resentful afterward that you didn't have any down time. The next time a friend asks for a weekend favor, check your energy levels first. If you are overflowing, go for it. If you feel depleted, let them know you are not available.

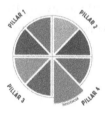

Influencer: Here's a wonderful chance for you to lead by example! In our hustle culture, we often see praise for influencers who relentlessly pursue goals and crush to-do lists, but that's not all there is to success. Success also comes with rest and recovery. We have energetic ebbs and flows. Some people are jazzed in the morning and fizzle out by the evening while some have an energetic slow start and are most productive at night. Our energy can flow by seasons, the time of school year, and by our bodies' natural ageing process. Be mindful of when you are most energetic and when you need to rest.

When others see you prioritizing rest, and yet being highly productive, you might just start a school-wide trend!

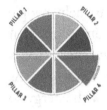

Nurturer: This chapter on rest might resonate with you, the Nurturer, the most nurturing of all the profiles! That's because you are self-aware and already know the value of self-care. Your challenge is to sustain this habit even when it's crunch time at work. Stopping to tend to your own needs is instrumental to your productivity, so remind yourself that not all work is the same – working when you're exhausted is painful, while working when rested can feel so much easier!

Your Thriving Road Map

Remember, rest is not just a break from productivity; it's the foundation of it. Write down your favorite key takeaway from this chapter and make a plan for how you will build rest into your day and/or create a post-work ritual.

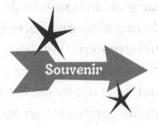

Write down one micro-habit strategy from this chapter that you want to take with you as a souvenir for yourself.

Write down one micro-habit strategy from this chapter that you want to take with you as a souvenir to use at your school or with your students.

Discussion Questions:

1. **Reflecting on Rest Patterns:** Reflect on your current patterns of rest. What does your "rearview mirror" show about the quality and quantity of your rest in the past few months? How does this awareness shape your Thriving Road Map for the future?

2. **Downtime as a Productivity Tool:** How can you reconceptualize rest and downtime as essential tools for your productivity, rather than as rewards for completing tasks? How might this shift in perspective change the way you plot out rest stops on your Thriving Road Map?

3. **Building Effective Rest Strategies:** What practical strategies can you incorporate into your daily routine to ensure that rest is effectively used as a catalyst for productivity and creativity? Are you currently prioritizing sleep and incorporating movement into the day? When you do, how does it affect your teaching and personal life? What small changes might you make to enhance these areas further?

4. **Balancing Rest and Work:** Discuss the challenges of finding time to rest during the school year. How can you plan for and protect this downtime without feeling guilty about the ongoing demands of teaching?

5. **Post-Work Detox Rituals:** Share a post-work detox ritual that helps you transition from work mode to relaxation. If you don't currently have a ritual, what is a daily routine you

would like to start? Is there anyone in your support network who can help with this practice?

6. **Your Personal Road Map:** Using your Thriving Road Map from Appendix A as a guide, what is one action step you can take immediately to cultivate more work-life alliance? What were your "souvenir" ideas you want to share with students?

Notes

1. Alex Soojung-Kim Pang (2017). How Resting More Can Boost Your Productivity. *Greater Good Magazine.* https://greatergood.berkeley.edu/article/item/how_resting_more_can_boost_your_productivity

2. Cara Palmer (2023). Sleep deprivation makes us less happy, more anxious. *American Psychological Association.* https://www.apa.org/news/press/releases/2023/12/sleep-deprivation-anxious?utm_source=linkedin&utm_medium=social&utm_campaign=apa-press-release-research&utm_content=dec21-sleep-deprivation

3. Eti Ben-Simon, Ph.D. (2023). The Damage Done by Just One Sleepless Night. *Psychology Today.* https://www.psychologytoday.com/intl/blog/sleep-talking/202312/how-does-one-sleepless-night-change-how-we-feel?utm_source=FacebookPost&utm_medium=FBPost&utm_campaign=FBPost&fbclid=IwAR38SMoBZvLkfwt25PrEMeYq4nCohG-9eZ5Jn8d_5WHBaMFkA5C0ROlvqIo_aem_AcW1YQJ74UpRfCicpm3k8rQYkCHK9zwt0XQ5lmzsQvAIlFXBxfMIMW8ZcLP7Ya-W0Ledsd3kxzYHuRr6jxSIRyRR

4. Matthew Ganio, Lawrence E. Armstrong, Douglas J. Casea, Brendon P. McDermott et al. (2011) "Mild Dehydrations Impairs Cognitive Performance and Mood of Men," *British Journal of Nutrition* 106, no. 10, pp. 1535-1543.

5. Jessica Stillman (2019). Neuroscientist: Walking Is a 'Superpower' That Makes Us Smarter, Healthier, and Happier. *Inc.* https://www.inc.com/jessica-stillman/neuroscientist-walking-is-a-superpower-that-makes-us-smarter-healthier-happier.html

6. Kendra Cherry, MSEd (2023). What Does the Color Green Mean? Very Well Mind. https://www.verywellmind.com/color-psychology-green-2795817#citation-3

7. Rachel Bachman (2017). How Close Do You Need to be to Your Gym? *The Wall Street Journal.* https://www.wsj.com/articles/how-close-do-you-need-to-be-to-your-gym-1490111186

CHAPTER

7

Cultivate Healthy Boundaries

"A river without boundaries is a swamp."

–Unknown

This chapter focuses on cultivating healthy boundaries. To continue our metaphor, it's about staying in your lane and helping others stay in theirs. As educators, this topic is vital in preventing burnout. In my experience and through my work with numerous school psychologists across the country, I've realized that cultivating healthy boundaries, especially in the helping professions, can be quite challenging. But it's not just about work-life boundaries; it extends to various aspects crucial for preserving your positive energy, physical energy, and headspace during the work day. Let's start with a reflection.

How do you feel when you say no? _____

Answers to this vary from "guilty" and "anxious" to "empowered." Typically, when I ask this question of educators, the scales tip toward negative emotions. When we, the helpers, say no to something, it can trigger us to feel badly for not being able to help. Or we feel anxious about saying no because someone in a position of authority is asking us, or we feel like we're going to be perceived as selfish, and not a team player. These negative emotions are only made worse if someone pushes back or expresses disappointment when we do get the courage to set a boundary.

In a field where there are inevitably more demands than time to fulfill them, how can we navigate the windy road and stay firm in our lane of balancing our needs with the needs of our school? Let's dig into why healthy boundaries, though sometimes difficult to set and hold, are essential for your well-being and sustainability in your career.

Why Boundaries Are Important for Burnout Prevention

Educators and other helping professionals are at a higher risk of burnout due to the nature of their jobs, which often involves constant giving. In fact, K-12 workers in the United States have the highest burnout rate of all industries nationally![1] Yikes!

Given this reality, what's the antidote? Part of the balm for this epidemic lies in self-awareness and understanding your role in the larger context of your work environment. Knowing yourself and your boundaries is crucial to prevent physical and emotional exhaustion.

Boundaries are not just rigid lines in the sand; they vary in their nature. They can be permeable, easily changed based on our mood or circumstances. I call these a "knee jerk yes" because someone asks, and our instinct is to say yes with no consideration of our own needs. Early career educators are particularly susceptible to this phenomenon since it's not always clear what is and isn't in the job description. Or when you set a boundary, at the first sign of push back or trying to convince you, you cave, for fear of disapproval or to avoid a conflict. However, research shows that these types of blurred boundaries often lead to reduced well-being.[2]

On the other hand, healthy boundaries, characterized by direct, open, and honest feedback about your limits, are linked with less frustration, anger, resentment, and burnout. What's more, is that people actually respect you more when you have clear boundaries.[3] Healthy boundaries not only benefit you but also your relationships. People don't have to like your boundaries, but they can respect them. Setting clear boundaries helps in building trust and healthier interactions with others.

Rigid boundaries, the "hard no," also have their place. These vary by person and situation, but you probably have a short list of things you will not do, and you already know this about yourself, so it's easy to say no. These rigid boundaries are important when it comes to personal safety, protecting sacred time off, and tending to your primary needs. Some rigid boundaries have their place, but the key here is to strive for balanced, healthy boundaries.

Here's another way to think about healthy boundaries: *Healthy boundaries are a form of self-compassion.* Dr. Kristin Neff's research highlights that self-compassion is more than just being kind to yourself; it's about empowering yourself through setting boundaries. She refers to this type of self-compassion as "fierce self-compassion" and her research shows that having both the tender and fierce sides of the equation promotes well-being, reduces depression and anxiety, and improves your relationships.[4] On a practical level, think of boundaries as self-compassion in this way: A strategic "no" is essentially an intentional "yes" to your well-being and priorities.

Bridging the Research to Your Reality

You might be saying to yourself, "Okay, okay, I get it, boundaries are important, but how do I actually set them and follow through without the guilt or anxiety about the conflict it may cause?" Let's turn to micro steps.

Starting with Yourself

Setting boundaries is a skill that needs to be practiced and communicated. Often, our default mode is to say yes without considering our own needs. This can lead to feelings of resentment and anger. To set effective boundaries, we must first be self-aware and understand our limits.

Here's the clincher that took me far too long to learn: to set healthy boundaries, you have to get clear *with yourself first*. It's much easier to say no to someone else's demand if you already know it's a hard no for you. If you've already pre-committed to leaving the building at 4 p.m. every day, it won't be as hard of a decision to say no to a 4 p.m. extra meeting. Half the boundary is set within yourself before anyone asks anything of you.

If you have a hard time saying no in the moment, buy yourself some time! Write down a script on a Post-it in your calendar that you can refer to and commit to memory, like "Let me think about it and get back to you by the end of the day" or "Let me look at my calendar and see if I have any moveable priorities or not." Then you can make a strategic choice from there, instead of a knee-jerk yes that you will later regret and be resentful. If the ask is something you do not have time for, you might frame it later as, "I have X and Y, and you've asked me to also do Z. What is your priority? What can be deprioritized for now?" This shows that you have limited time in the day, but you are responsive to their priorities.

It's always a little trickier when you have asks from your supervisor or "higher ups" because saying no to something could be seen as insubordination. In these situations, you can ask, "Is this something I am allowed to think about?" Or, "Am I allowed to say no to this?" and then you will know if it's a must do or simply an ask. If it is something that is a must do that adds something to your plate, then you can start from there and negotiate other things to be removed from your plate (e.g. "If I am required to do morning bus duty every day, would it be possible to be relieved of recess duty to recover the prep time I need to create effective and engaging lessons for my students?").

Micro Boundaries: Small Steps Toward Big Change

Consider setting micro boundaries, small steps that are manageable and can be a starting point for bigger changes. These could be personal boundaries you set for yourself or with others, like ensuring you take a lunch break without distractions, closing and locking your door during your prep period so you get the protected and focused time you need, or asking for a 15-minute buffer time to reboot in between parent meetings.

Start with a small, non-negotiable boundary for yourself, something that you strictly adhere to. This could be as simple as not working through your lunch break. Once laptop free lunch becomes a habit, you can gradually move toward more flexible boundaries. The key is to make mindful choices.

I'd be remiss if I didn't talk about tech boundaries! Our "always on" culture makes it all too easy to have permeable boundaries for checking email after work or bringing home your laptop to "get caught up" or to prepare for the next day. The first step in change is to contemplate what changes you would like to make with tech. The next step is to commit to them.

Let's say you no longer want to respond to emails during non-school hours. But maybe you're not ready to go "cold turkey" because you have a worry that you will miss something important, or you will get backlogged and never be able to dig out of your inbox ever again if you don't keep on top of it.

Start small by adding some friction to the habit of checking email. Here are some tips:

- Take your work email off your phone.
- Remove email alerts, which tempt you to check.
- If you aren't ready to remove work email from your phone, put it on the last page of your phone app screen. If you're checking, it's a conscious choice because you have to swipe three times to make it happen.
- Leave your laptop at work altogether.
- Leave your laptop charger at work, so you are forced to limit your time on your work computer.
- Put a hair scrunchie or elastic band on your phone to block facial recognition. Take a mindful pause before you remove the band to get into your phone and ask yourself why you are checking your phone. Getting a recommendation for good take-out? Proceed! Bored and want to see who emailed you? Decide if you want to proceed *mindfully*.

Handling Pushbacks on Boundaries

Angela Watson, my co-passenger teacher buddy on the road to Thrive Town, has some great insights on boundaries. If you haven't read every single one of her books or listened to her podcast, *Truth For Teachers*, you're in for a treat – she's full of boundary-setting ideas! Here are just a few of her pearls of wisdom from our *Reverse Educator Burnout* course:

- **Boundaries are not ultimatums.** They aren't things you try to force other people to do. Since you can't control anyone's behavior but your own, you can't create a boundary that will only be effective if other people change.

- **A proper boundary is an action you choose to take to protect yourself.** It's based on your own actions: If X happens, I will do Y (e.g. If a parent emails during non-work hours, my auto-responder will provide them with a message that I received their email and I will respond during school hours).

- **Don't expect people to stop asking you to take more things on.** Expecting other people to change their behavior will often create frustration and strained relationships. The boundary is that YOU will say no (e.g. If the boundary is not emailing on weekends, you no longer have to waste any of your precious energy getting annoyed if a parent does that. They can email you, but you just don't respond until Monday.).

Remember, those who get most upset about your boundaries are often the ones used to violating them. It's natural to encounter some resistance, but staying true to your known limits is essential for your well-being and preventing burnout. Give yourself permission to set boundaries, especially if you know that they will help you do your job more effectively, protect your downtime to rejuvenate (Chapter 6!), or allow you to take better care of yourself.

Micro-Habits to Use Your
Thrive-O-Gram Strength

As we wrap up this module, I encourage you to reflect on what healthy boundaries look like for you. Embrace the understanding that maintaining healthy boundaries is not just beneficial for you but is also a cornerstone in building trustful and respectful relationships, both personally and professionally. Keep in mind that setting boundaries is a form of self-care and a step toward a healthier, more balanced life.

I wish there was a simple habit hack to be able to consistently set boundaries without guilt. While I've offered some practical suggestions in this chapter, living a life with healthy boundaries requires a bit more work than say, changing a behavior that isn't so emotionally charged, like drinking more water in the day. There's often a subconscious reason we say yes to things we want to say no to.

For example, if you grew up in a home where you were taught to respect authority and your needs weren't validated, saying no can trigger a fear that you will somehow get "in trouble" or "make someone angry." If guilt and shame was prevalent in your upbringing, saying no might be hard for you because you don't want to disappoint anyone or feel shame. In yet other situations, you might not have had any modeling of how to set healthy boundaries. These experiences are carried with us into the workplace. Left unexamined, these underlying beliefs about what it means to set a boundary can override even the best of boundary-setting intentions. Participating in therapy, coaching, or reading books on healthy boundaries can be an intervention that has multiple benefits.

With this in mind, the following suggestions, based on your Thrive-o-gram strengths profile, include a behavioral step you can take as well as a mantra that might help you in your journey to setting healthy boundaries.

 **Go-Getter:** As someone who loves to accomplish tasks, cross off to-do list items, and generally strive for achievement, you might struggle with saying no because you genuinely love to feel accomplished by doing. Your boundary-setting mantra: "I can do anything, but I do not have to do *everything*."

 **Fascinator:** As someone with a genuine interest in learning new things, you might struggle with saying no because it could be a good learning opportunity. Your boundary setting mantra: "Saying no to this opportunity now protects my energy. There will always be new opportunities to say yes to in the future."

 **Creator:** You may struggle with saying no because you love to take on new ideas and initiatives. Your boundary-setting mantra: "I do not have to do the whole world right now. Focusing my energy on a few initiatives will keep me from being spread too thin."

 **Architect:** As an architect, you might see how others' asking you to do something fits into a larger picture and have a hard time saying no because you can imagine the value your contribution may add. Your boundary-setting mantra: "An intentional no creates opportunities for a strategic yes."

 **Connector:** As someone who values connecting and collaborating with others, it may be difficult to say no to a colleague, especially if you are good friends with them and value their ideas. Your boundary-setting mantra: "A respectful no prevents a resentful yes."

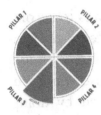

Helper: Putting others' needs before your own is a common trap for the Helper. However, protecting your energy now allows for you to give more help later. Your boundary-setting mantra: "It's not self-centered to be centered in myself first."

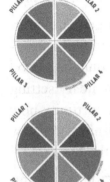

Influencer: Harness that fierce self-compassion energy, Influencer! Your boundary-setting mantra: "Saying no is a healthy form of self-care."

Nurturer: Self-compassion is one of your core strengths, so tap into that when you are faced with having to set boundaries with yourself and others. Your boundary-setting mantra: "I can nurture myself first to have the energy to nurture others."

Your Thriving Road Map

Remember: healthy boundaries start with knowing yourself! Write down your favorite key takeaway from this chapter and decide which healthy boundary you'd like to start cultivating or reinforcing today!

Write down one micro-habit strategy from this chapter that you want to take with you as a souvenir for yourself.

Write down one micro-habit strategy from this chapter that you want to take with you as a souvenir to use at your school or with your students.

Discussion Questions:

1. **Boundary Setting in Action:** Share an experience where you successfully set a boundary in your professional life. What strategies helped you maintain this boundary, and how did it impact your well-being and work relationships?

2. **Responding to Pushback:** Boundaries often come with resistance. Can you recall a time when someone didn't respect your boundary? How did you handle it, and what did you learn from that experience?

3. **Cultivating Self-Awareness:** How does self-awareness play a role in setting and maintaining healthy boundaries? What are some steps you can take to become more self-aware in your professional interactions?

4. **The Guilt of "No":** What are the emotions that come up for you when you say "no?" Discuss ways we can navigate these feelings to stay true to our boundaries.

5. **Micro-Boundary Strategies:** Think of a "micro-boundary" you can set this week. What is a small step you can take that respects your limits and helps preserve your energy? Write down a "script" for setting this boundary, such as "I attend meetings during my contract hours" or "I cannot commit to this extra project" and practice saying it with confidence and conviction with a partner. How does it feel to say this boundary out loud?

6. **Your Personal Road Map:** Using your Thriving Road Map from Appendix A as a guide, what is one action step you can take immediately to cultivate more work-life alliance? What were your "souvenir" ideas you want to share with students?

Notes

1. Stephanie Marken and Sangeeta Agrawal (2022). K–12 Workers Have Highest Burnout Rate in U.S. *Gallup*. https://news.gallup.com/poll/393500/workers-highest-burnout-rate.aspx
2. Helen Pluut and Jaap Wonders (2020). Not Able to Lead a Healthy Life When You Need It the Most: Dual Role of Lifestyle Behaviors in the Association of Blurred Work-Life Boundaries With Well-Being. *Frontiers in Psychology*. https://www.ncbi.nlm.nih.gov/pmc/articles/PMC7786197/
3. Nedra Glover Tawwab (2021). *Set Boundaries, Find Peace: A Guide to Reclaiming Yourself*. New York: TarcherPerigee.
4. Kristin Neff (2011). *Self-Compassion: The Proven Power of Being Kind to Yourself*. New York: William Morrow.

8

Reduce Daily Stress

"My job is all consuming. I feel like it bleeds into my personal life. I want to change that, but it feels hard. Daily, I am stressed leaving work. I am 25 years old and don't want to feel this way until I retire. I also don't want to leave the profession of teaching either. I'm stuck!"

—Anonymous

What is the first thing that comes to mind when we think of an antidote to stress? Chances are, most people say "self-care." The thing is, lately I've noticed that if I say "self-care" in a training on educator burnout, there's a collective eye roll among educators in the room, as if to say, "Oh great, here we go again with the self-care stuff. As if I have time for *that*."

It's not that educators don't think self-care is important; it's that self-care has been weaponized in our society to suggest that burnout is a *worker* issue, not a *workplace* issue. But burnout isn't a personal "self-care fail"! Self-care interventions, in isolation, imply that we're just not taking enough yoga classes or meditating enough to cope with the stress.

Self-care is a *downstream* intervention after the stress has already happened. It's important and useful, but we also need to look *upstream* to the systemic forces at work that are causing the stress in the first place.

And, crucially, self-care needs to be coupled with practicing self-compassion that *we are doing our best* in a stressful system.

So, what are some of these upstream challenges? I recently polled my Thriving Students Collective community of teachers, school psychologists, and other K–12 educators on social media about the top sources of stress. Here's what made the top five:

- Time spent in administrative tasks
- Lack of time to prep or work on desired tasks
- Lack of support/understanding from administration
- Lack of resources to support neurodivergent students
- Lack of resources to support students with mental health issues

I then asked what is one thing that would reduce stress. It was eye opening that the interventions were largely doable, not sweeping policy changes or massive funding efforts that would rock the landscape of education as we know it. It was things like administration honoring and protecting prep time, more humanity, more compassion and understanding from administration, and support for students with challenges. Turns out, we can give ourselves much of what we seek from others, with healthy boundaries, self-compassion, and leveling up our skills to work with diverse populations of students.

In the reality of increasing student needs and educators' decreasing emotional bandwidth from the stress of it all, how can we address the upstream issues while tending to our own needs downstream? First, let's look at the connection between stress and positive growth.

Why Reducing Daily Stress Is Essential for Burnout Prevention

Reducing stress is a critical part of our journey toward thriving as educators. We learned in previous chapters that chronic stress leads to a whole host of health and well-being challenges. Research also shows that even the small daily hassles can accumulate to big stress and burnout.[1] The good news is, the flip side is also true: If we tackle the small things in our control, we can make big changes in our stress.

Remember from Chapter 5 "Reduce Frustration" that stress is not always a bad thing – it's only when it is chronic and unchecked that it becomes problematic. While stress can be overwhelming, remember that navigating through it can lead to "post-traumatic growth." Just as we guide students to overcome challenges by turning them into opportunities for emotional and intellectual growth, we can do the same for ourselves.

Before we dive in, let's do a brief reflection. I want you to imagine that a teacher comes to you at the end of the day for support. She had a terrible day – kids were acting out, she got a harsh and critical email from a parent because she was too busy to respond to a previous email, and she didn't get to eat her lunch because she was supporting a student in crisis. She is planning to stay late to prepare for tomorrow, but she's feeling exhausted. What do you say to her?

If a friend was struggling, I would say: _____.

Now, read what you wrote and ask yourself, "Is this the same advice I tell myself when I am in a similar situation?" Chances are, what you wrote to comfort your friend is kind and compassionate, and what you tell yourself on most days is much more critical (e.g. "Ugh, why didn't I reply to that parent? That wasn't very smart, I should have known better! And I should have handled that behavioral issue better, then I would have been able to eat lunch."). And yet, you'd never tell a friend, "Why didn't you reply to that parent? That wasn't very smart, you should have known better!" I mean, not if you want to keep your friends! And yet, we say unkind things to ourselves all the time, and barely even notice we are doing it.

Enter the biggest stress-busting concept you will learn in this book for challenges big and small: Self-compassion.

Self-compassion involves treating ourselves with the same kindness, concern, and support we would offer to a good friend. Kristin Neff is a leading researcher in the field of self-compassion, and her findings emphasize the profound impact of self-compassion on mental and physical well-being. Self-compassion has been shown to reduce depression and anxiety, improve health and immunity, build resilience, enhance persistence, and improve happiness.[2] Notably, this is done without removing the stressor, but rather reacting to it in a self-compassionate way.

Here's how it works in action: The practice of self-compassion, as explained by Neff, is not just about being kind to ourselves but also involves recognizing our shared humanity and maintaining a balanced awareness of our emotions in the following three ways:

1. **Self-Kindness vs. Self-Judgment:** This aspect involves being gentle and understanding with ourselves rather than

harshly critical. We listen in and check that the language we are using when we fall short, encounter a stressor, or have a hard day is kind. It's about cultivating a strong inner best friend to talk to you, rather than listening to a strong inner critic.

2. **Common Humanity vs. Isolation:** This recognizes that suffering and personal inadequacy are part of the shared human experience. You are not the only educator to get a harsh email or make a mistake with classroom management. Nothing has gone wrong; this is part of being an educator. This is comforting to remember in times of stress.

3. **Mindfulness vs. Over-Identification:** This involves a balanced approach to our negative emotions so that we neither suppress nor exaggerate them. We can name our emotions (remember name it to tame it?) and allow them, as they are. We turn to them and say, "Hello, shame/annoyance/anger, I see you. It makes sense why you are here." The feeling will pass, if we don't continue to throw fuel on the emotional fire with our thoughts ("I can't believe this parent! Who do they think they are? It's so unfair!").

In the throes of a stressful moment, practice self-compassion by acknowledging your feelings, reminding yourself you are not alone, and then treating yourself as you would a close friend. The beauty of self-compassion is it's a skill that can be practiced anywhere, especially in the moment, when you are encountering a stressful situation at work.

Bridging the Research to Your Reality

Here's where I'm finally going to mention the S-word: "self-care." But don't worry, I'm not going to suggest that a bubble bath will solve all your problems. It's more about the thought bubbles in your mind that precede and support the self-care behaviors.

Self-Care and Self-Compassion: Companions in Wellness

There is an interconnection between self-care and self-compassion. People who practice self-compassion do more self-care behaviors. Why is this?

First, when you practice self-compassion, you are being present with your stress, rather than fighting or ruminating over it, which buffers against burnout. This practice involves acknowledging stress as a temporary state and using it as an opportunity to be aware of our options and values. It cultivates an "inner pause button," enabling us to make conscious choices based on our current situation and values.

That conscious choice is to treat yourself like you would a best friend. On the job, that looks like speaking to yourself with self-compassion in the moment of stress. Off the job, that looks like practicing self-care behaviors, which are important for completing the "stress cycle."

Complete the Stress Cycle

I hate to break it to you, but rarely is there going to be a day without a stressor. And if you vanquish one stressor today, chances are, another different stressor will pop up tomorrow. You might make a breakthrough with an unhappy parent today, and then the next day, a student has an unexpected blowout in your class. The goal is not to eradicate stress; the goal is to find ways to cope with it, learn from it, and grow your educator toolkit to be prepared the next time something crops up.

The problem is, so many of us are walking around with unprocessed stress. We handle the stressor in the moment, but our nervous systems still hold onto the stress, and it accumulates.

As far as our amygdala (the fear center of our brain) is concerned, modern day stressors like harsh emails and kids acting out are registered in the same way as primitive stressors, like encountering saber-tooth tigers. Our brain, doing its delightful job of keeping us safe, sends out stress hormones. In nature, the stress hormones subside when the threat is gone. But we experience modern-day threats every day. So, working in a stressful environment is like meeting a new saber-tooth tiger every day, but we hold onto the stress hormones because we never feel safe to let down our guard.

So how do we process the stress in an environment of perpetual stressors? We do so by completing the stress cycle.[3] After a stressful event, we find a way to let our bodies know we are safe again. This closes the loop, and our stress hormones return to baseline. Here are seven ways that Emily and Amelia Nagoski, authors of *Burnout: The Secret to Unlocking the Stress Cycle*, suggest to complete the cycle:

1. **Exercise Regularly:** Incorporate physical activities like running, dancing, or swimming into your daily routine for 20 to 60 minutes to combat stress.

2. **Practice Deep Breathing:** Simple breathwork like taking a four count inhale and an eight count exhale can calm the stress response. Ideally, deep breathing methods should be no less than 90 seconds for benefits.

3. **Engage in Social Interactions:** Even small, friendly exchanges with people, like complimenting a barista, can signal safety and normalcy to your stressed brain.

4. **Laugh Wholeheartedly:** Share deep, genuine laughs to release stress and strengthen social bonds.

5. **Connect with Loved Ones:** Deepen your connections with those you trust; even hugs longer than a few seconds with a friend or partner can be soothing.

6. **Allow Yourself to Cry:** Crying can help process and relieve stress, even if the situation causing it remains unchanged.

7. **Be Creative:** Engage in creative activities to foster positive emotions and energy for the following day.

Herein, you can see the neurological value in self-care. These self-care behaviors complete the stress cycle. I have personally picked my three favorites – exercise, be creative, and engage in social interactions, and turned it into a mantra to remind myself of how to complete the stress cycle: "Move my body, do a thing, or be with a person." Pick a few you love and make it into your mantra!

Finding Your Self-Care Language

One of the reasons people might bristle against the idea of self-care is they are thinking only about one brand of self-care, the yoga-going or working out at the gym side of self-care. The truth is, there are many ways to practice self-care, and you need to find the flavor of self-care that works for you.

Have you ever heard of the concept of Love Languages? It's the idea that we give and receive love differently, and it's often used in couples therapy to help with connection. For example, one person in a relationship feels loved when their partner says, "I love you"; the other person might feel loved when someone spends quality time with them or gives them physical affection. Knowing this about your partner, you can better understand personal needs in relationships.

Applying this concept to self-care involves recognizing what actions or gestures make *you* feel cared for and rejuvenated. The key is to know yourself and your needs well. Just as love languages guide us in understanding how to express care in relationships, self-care languages focus on identifying what actions make us feel nurtured and supported personally (see Figure 8.1). So, what is your self-care language?

- Words of Affirmation:
  - Self-Dialogue: Incorporating positive self-talk and affirmations into your daily routine.
  - Journaling: Writing down thoughts and affirmations to reinforce self-love and appreciation.
- Acts of Service:
  - Self-Management: Tasks like scheduling appointments, organizing your space, or completing personal to-do lists.
  - Self-Care Rituals: Establishing routines such as skincare, a nutritious diet, or setting aside time for relaxation.
- Receiving Gifts:
  - Treating Yourself: Indulging in small luxuries, like buying a book, a craft kit, or planning a staycation.
  - Experiences: Prioritizing spending on experiences that bring joy, such as attending a workshop or a short trip.
- Physical Touch:
  - Movement and Exercise: Engaging in activities like yoga, stretching, or sports that make the body feel good.
  - Comfort through Touch: Wearing comfortable clothes, cuddling under a cozy blanket, or getting a massage.
- Quality Time (Me Time and We Time):
  - Me Time: Activities like meditation, reading, or solitary drives (Thrive Drive), allowing for self-reflection and peace.
  - We Time: Fun activities with friends or family, like dinner outings, happy hours, or group hobbies.
  - Fun and Play: Engaging in activities that are playful and induce a state of flow, either alone or with others.

FIGURE 8.1 Self-care languages

Select the self-care practices that feel most soothing, fun, restorative, or empowering to you.

Be aware that your self-care needs may evolve. What felt restorative at one point in life may change, and it's important to adapt accordingly. The next step is to integrate these self-care practices into your everyday life to ensure a consistent nurturing of your well-being, through incorporating self-care into your routine, like scheduling regular social events or activities that rejuvenate you, and regularly reflecting on what acts of self-care you can commit to each week and make conscious efforts to follow through.

Remember that it's not self-centered to be centered in yourself (full credit to my therapist for this gem of a quote!). Self-care does not mean you're selfish. We know from the research that when you are emotionally regulated, your students benefit.[4] We also know that when we are stressed, we are more likely to act on our implicit biases, so reducing your stress has an added benefit for your equity practices.[5]

Look Upstream

While self-compassion and self-care can help with daily stress, it's important to also look "upstream" to the constant stressors and get creative about how to address them. What are the "saber-tooth tigers" in your day? What are the systemic things that constantly contribute to your stress?

For many educators, it's the rising needs of the students and the lack of training or supports to serve them effectively. The reality is that one in five students has a diagnosed learning or attention disability, and students spend 80% of their days in general education classrooms.[6] That data doesn't even include *undiagnosed* disabilities or students with mental health issues, like anxiety or depression. In today's schools, all educators are special educators.

The challenge is, only 17% of general education teachers feel equipped to support students with mild or moderate disabilities.[7] Many educators did not get adequate training in how to teach complex learners in their certification programs, and ongoing professional development isn't keeping pace with how to address your students' needs *today*. So, if you're a general education teacher, odds are, one of your upstream issues is the efficacy gap between what your students need and your skillset to support them.

If you want immediate support, feel free to check out my Thrive Hive TV network, which provides short, research-backed strategies from trusted experts to level up your skills in supporting students with disabilities and mental health needs in the classroom.

www.thrivingstudents.com/thrive-hive

Micro-Habits to Use Your
Thrive-O-Gram Strength

As educators, practicing self-compassion is not only about being kind to ourselves but also about setting an example for our students. By adopting a mindful approach to our own well-being, we can create a more positive and nurturing environment for those we teach. When we stop to correct our inner critic to be an inner bestie, we can significantly change our relationship to stress. And when we model this process for our students, we give them the gift of learning how to cultivate self-compassion, too.

When it comes to self-care and closing the stress cycle, my fabulous co-passenger Angela Watson reminds us: *Consistency is more important than intensity.* Choose one or two strategies from the self-care language categories that resonate with you. Embed these small self-care practices into your daily routine for consistent well-being improvement. And remember, the goal is to make self-care a regular and manageable part of your daily life, not an occasional grand gesture. By integrating these simple, yet effective self-care strategies into your routine, you create a sustainable path to personal well-being and professional fulfillment.

Here's some fun research on how to build consistency with a new habit. It sounds so simple, but here it is: write it down. Yep, just writing down your goals increases likelihood you will follow through.[8] This is because you have pre-committed yourself. For extra bonus, also pre-plan for obstacles and how you will overcome them (e.g. I will take an afternoon run on Monday. If it is raining, I will do a YouTube video. If I'm too tired, I will take a walk instead of a run).

Let's turn to more ways you can turn your Thrive-o-gram strengths into a source for resilience and growth.

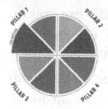 **Go-Getter:** Get ready to populate your to-do list with self-care! Schedule one thing per day that feels restorative to you. If you forget to do it, reschedule it, just like you would reschedule a missed dentist appointment. Challenge yourself to see how long of a self-care streak you can achieve!

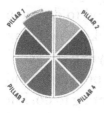 **Fascinator:** You love to dig deep, so let's find that one thing that you would love to spend time doing. Think about it this way: If you had an extra eighth day of the week where you could do anything restorative or fun, no other obligations in sight, what would it be? Look at your calendar and carve out time for it!

 **Creator:** I bet you can get creative about figuring out ways to fold self-care into your day! Make a vision board? An elaborate wall calendar of Post-its? A self-care menu that you choose from every day after work? Choose your own self-care adventure!

 **Architect:** What self-care strategy can you build from the ground up, architect? What's your foundation? This might be a keystone habit, like getting 7-8 hours of sleep, or 20 minutes of walking every day. Keystone habits are ones that when you master them, other habits fall into place (like good sleep gives you more energy for working out, or walking every day makes you more conscious of limiting your sugar intake).

Connector: What self-care rituals can you do with others? Mid-day dance or stretching break with your students? Walking with a friend after work? Taking a cooking class with your partner? Pick one that you want to try this week and find a buddy to commit with you.

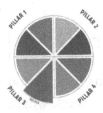

Helper: Turn your love of helping others on yourself! Maybe it will feel good to do some acts of service for yourself, like scheduling that doctor's appointment for yourself you've been putting off or finishing a project around the house that you've been wanting to do. Put acts of helping yourself on your calendar and commit to them just like you would for others.

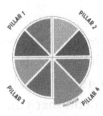

Influencer: Have a long lost hobby or activity you'd like to pick up again? Think about what you loved to do as a child – wander around in nature? Tap dance? Soccer? Dedicate an hour a week to this hobby to close the stress cycle, and you'll be influencing others to do the same, by example!

Nurturer: Set a self-care intention each morning, perhaps by pairing it with a morning cup of coffee or tea. As you sip, think of one thing you can do that day that would feel nurturing or restorative. Put the idea on a Post-it and put it somewhere you will see it (e.g. a planner, on your counter when you get home) and be reminded of your intention.

Your Thriving Road Map

Remember: Treat yourself like you would a best friend! Write down your favorite key takeaway from this chapter and decide on the self-compassionate mindset and self-care behaviors you'd like to start cultivating or reinforcing today!

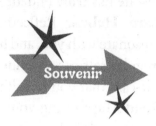

Write down one micro-habit strategy from this chapter that you want to take with you as a souvenir for yourself.

Write down one micro-habit strategy from this chapter that you want to take with you as a souvenir to use at your school or with your students.

Discussion Questions:

1. **Navigating Work-Life Balance:** How do you create separation between your work life and personal life? What strategies have you found effective in ensuring that stress from work does not seep into your personal time?

2. **Self-Compassion Practices:** Can you share a personal experience where treating yourself with kindness and understanding helped you through a stressful situation at work? Do you have a "fierce" self-compassion moment where you tended to your self-care by saying no? How did that feel? What can you learn from your previous experience that you want to continue in the future?

3. **Identifying Stressors:** What are some daily stressors that you face in your role, and what are the "upstream" factors contributing to these stressors? How can you address them proactively? What advice would you give a best educator friend if they were in the same situation?

4. **Completing the Stress Cycle:** Discuss methods you use to complete the stress cycle. What activities help you to feel that a stressful episode has truly ended?

5. **Building Self-Care Habits:** Reflecting on the self-care languages, which resonate with you, and how can you incorporate them into a regular self-care routine? What's one micro-habit related to self-care that you're willing to start today?

6. **Your Personal Road Map:** Using your Thriving Road Map from Appendix A as a guide, what is one action step you can take immediately to cultivate more work-life alliance? What were your "souvenir" ideas you want to share with students?

Notes

1. Rob Cross and Karen Dillon (2024). The Hidden Toll of Microstress. *HBR* Special Issues, Spring 2024, pp. 10-18
2. Kristin Neff (2011). *Self-Compassion: The Proven Power of Being Kind to Yourself.* New York: William Morrow.
3. Emily Nagoski, PhD and Amelia Nagoski, DMA (2019). *Burnout: The Secret to Unlocking the Stress Cycle.* New York: Ballantine Books.
4. Leanne Fried (2011). Teaching Teachers about Emotion Regulation in the Classroom. *Australian Journal of Education.* https://files.eric.ed.gov/fulltext/EJ920029.pdf
5. Jackie Murphy et al. (2023). Mindfulness as a self-care strategy for healthcare professionals to reduce stress and implicit bias. *Journal of Interprofessional Education & Practice* March 2023, 100598. https://www.sciencedirect.com/science/article/abs/pii/S2405452622001057#:~:text=Increased%20levels%20of%20stress%20can,outcomes%20resulting%20in%20healthcare%20disparities
6. National Center for Education Statistics (2023). Students With Disabilities. *Condition of Education.* U.S. Department of Education, Institute of Education Sciences. Retrieved [date], from https://nces.ed.gov/programs/coe/indicator/cgg
7. Stacy Galiatsos et al. (2019). Forward Together: Helping Educators Unlock the Power of Students Who Learn Differently. National Center for Learning Disabilities. https://www.scribd.com/document/411837242/Forward-Together-NCLD-Report
8. Mark Murphy (2018). Neuroscience Explains Why You Need to Write Down Your Goals If You Actually Want to Achieve Them. *Forbes.* https://www.forbes.com/sites/markmurphy/2018/04/15/neuroscience-explains-why-you-need-to-write-down-your-goals-if-you-actually-want-to-achieve-them/?sh=797f4da87905

CHAPTER

9

Gratitude

"With so much negativity swirling around education, to keep positive at work, I just try to live in the little moments – that smile from a child, the adorable artwork my kids make, or even just having a warm classroom on a cold day. It makes the struggle all worth it."

—Kim, 2nd grade teacher

On our road trip to Thrive Town, you might be wondering, are we there yet?!? Not quite, but almost! But instead of speeding past everything to arrive at our destination, we're going to take the scenic route of gratitude! Gratitude is one of the clearest paths to reboot our passion on our journey to thriving, because it reminds us of all the reasons that we love being educators.

Before we get going, let's do a rearview mirror reflection. What comes to mind when you hear "gratitude practice?" Easy? Hard? Corny? Something you tried to do for a week in a gratitude journal and now the journal is sitting there, gathering dust? Let's do a practice together and see what comes up for you. Pause for a moment and jot down one thing you are grateful for.

I am grateful for _____

How hard was this for you? How long did it take for you to come up with something? Did you pick a big thing, like health or family? Or did you pick a small moment of gratitude?

I want to start this chapter by saying that gratitude doesn't have to be a big old monumental thing. As educators, rarely do we see the Hollywood moment where moving music plays and we get a crescendo moment where we get proof that we transformed a life through the power of teaching. You know that movie moment – when the struggle all becomes worth it, there's potentially a whole class slow clap of appreciation of the teacher, and we all cry tears of joy! Now, if you've been in education a while, you may have had a few of these grand moments (absent the moving soundtrack and slow clap) as students come back and share how you changed their lives. These moments are certainly to be cherished.

However, for most educators, it's not the big stuff we get to celebrate; it's the tiny moments. Small, seemingly insignificant moments stack up if we stop to notice them. Gratitude lives in the little moments, and it's fun to start savoring these moments! We'll explore specific practices later, but for now, remember, gratitude doesn't have to be only for monumental things.

Why Gratitude Is Important for Burnout Prevention

Gratitude literally changes the structure of your brain. It's fascinating! There are three key benefits around well-being, stress, and health that I want to highlight. Gratitude helps you feel positive emotions, relish good experiences, and build strong relationships. It boosts dopamine and serotonin, and keeps your gray matter functioning. In terms of stress, it shows reduced levels of depression, anxiety, and toxic emotions. Health benefits include lower blood pressure, less heart disease, better weight control, and healthier blood sugar levels.[1] Again, like mindfulness, if this were a pill, y'all would definitely be lining up at the pharmacy.

So, knowing the benefits, why aren't we all more grateful?

Our biology is the answer. We are evolutionarily programmed to scan for danger, so we need to train our brains to also scan for positive things. We tend to remember the negative things, because it helps us stay alive (thank you, brain!). And while we scan for physical danger, more commonly in the modern world, we scan for and lock in moments of *psychological danger* – is my principal upset with me? Did that lesson go well? Am I going to get a nasty-gram email for teaching about a sensitive topic? Did people like the way I presented at that IEP meeting?

So, at the end of the day, our default is to focus on the negative, even if we are fairly optimistic people. As one of my favorite quotes from Rick Hanson reads, "The brain is like Velcro for negative experiences but Teflon for positive ones." So, let's dig into some practical ways to Velcro the positive, too!

Bridging Research to Your Reality

I have to admit, I had a dusty gratitude journal on my bedside. I know the research on gratitude, so I bought it and imagined myself, curled up at night, lovingly reflecting on my day full of blessings. And then, every night, I looked at it and was too tired to write in it. So much for practicing what I preach!

It wasn't until I dug in a little more on the habit formation side of things that I was able to fold it more into my day. I used habit stacking, and paired my gratitude journal with my well-established morning routine of coffee and 10-minute mediation and just write down one thing I appreciate. At the end of the day, pair reviewing my to-do list for the next day with gratitude. Lo and behold, I am now grateful my gratitude journal doesn't have any dust on it! So let's dig into a few research to reality strategies that you might want to try on for size.

Savoring

Have you ever heard of rumination? This is the process where we think and rethink the same event over and over. Negative rumination, in the extreme, can be a symptom of depression. It's like getting stuck in the same negative feedback loop all day with your thinking patterns. For example, if you think, "Kids don't show me any respect these days" you might replay all the moments of disrespect from one of your students that day. And yet, with this mindset, you're also discounting the 25 students in your class who were respectful.

The antidote to rumination is savoring. It's thinking about the positive and reliving the pleasant moments, and it's been found to have several stress-busting benefits, including stronger relationships, improved mental and physical health, and the ability to find more creative solutions to problems.[2]

It's like when food is so good you stop, slow down, and savor each delicious bite. In the school day, what are the delicious moments you can savor and relive at the end of the day? For example, if you think, "I am teaching students to be respectful," you might replay all the tiny moments where you saw respect. From the student who helped you pick up a dropped pencil to a special breakthrough moment one-on-one with a child, or even just a funny moment in the class where everyone was having a great time. In the moment, when these positive things are happening, pay attention to them and savor them. This practice can help you reboot your passion because the moments remind you of why you became an educator in the first place.

Micro-Happiness

Teach yourself and your students to live in the little moments of gratitude. It doesn't have to be a big thing. These tiny moments stack up. The brain loves patterns, and you'll find it starts scanning for more tiny moments of positivity. Embed little gratitude moments in your day:

- Guide students in short experiential gratitude exercises, like looking out the window to appreciate nature, or taking a moment to think about something positive in their lives.

- Make it a habit to include gratitude in daily conversations, celebrating small wins like sunny weather for outdoor recess, rainy weather for a fun indoor recess, or a well-done task.

- Have students embed gratitude in writing tasks, like a daily or weekly gratitude journal.

- Pull out themes of gratitude from literature and discuss them in read-alouds.

- Create a gratitude wall of Post-its where students can share appreciations and happy moments from the day.

- Put a Post-it up in your room that says "Appreciate" and when you see it, take a moment to savor something good. Move the Post-it each day (or have your students move it!)

so it doesn't fade into the background and you start to ignore it. As you move around the room and spot the Post-it, you are reminded that gratitude is all around you.

Gratitude Journal

Gratitude journals and apps that prompt you to log what you are grateful for are classic examples of how to "Velcro" the positive in your day. Research shows that people who write in a gratitude journal weekly for 10 weeks or daily for 2 weeks experienced more gratitude, positive moods, and optimism about the future, as well as better sleep, compared to those who journal about hassles or their daily life.[3] If the word "gratitude" trips you up because it feels too lofty and big, try these sentence starters instead: "I appreciate . . ." or "One happy moment today was . . ."

Let's put a twist on the classic gratitude journal that may make it even easier to become a habit. Maybe you're like me – at the end of the day, I look at my to-do list and then I make a fresh one for the next day, based on everything I didn't get to. However, instead of focusing on the undone tasks on your to-do list, what if you also paired it with highlighting the small wins and moments of gratitude from your day? Turn your to-do list practice into a gratitude practice by savoring what you did accomplish (a "to-done" list! Or, as my school psych buddy calls it, her "ta-da!" list!). At the end of the day, instead of just moving on to creating your next to-do list, really savor what you did that day. Research shows this practice increases optimism, problem-solving challenges, and mood.[4]

Setting Intentions and Celebrating Small Wins

Research shows that people who have mentally prepared for and thought about the upcoming workday have a better work experience because they start the day off more in touch with their work goals.[5] So, can you mentally prepare for one thing you want to accomplish? One positive moment you want to strive for? Experiment with setting one intention at the beginning of the day that will make you feel good if you accomplish it. At the end of the day, reflect on it. If you achieved it, celebrate it! If you didn't get to it, reset the intention for the next day, and perhaps celebrate something else. Small wins and victories count!

Praise Prism

We've talked about internal gratitude practices, such as savoring and focusing on the good parts of your day, but what about external gratitude practices? Research shows that giving gratitude or praise to another has a triple benefit. The person who *gives* the gratitude feels good, the person *receiving* the gratitude feels good, and, notably, any person *witnessing* the exchange of gratitude also feels good.[6] Shawn Achor, author of *Big Potential*, calls this the "Praise Prism." Just as a prism reflects light out from three sides, these three benefits radiate out into your entire classroom or school community.

Micro-Habits to Use Your Thrive-O-Gram Strength

One of my favorite habit hacks is called *habit stacking*. Habit stacking is when you pair an established habit with something that is a new habit. You might call it the "something old, something new" plan. For example, hopefully, you have a habit of clicking your seatbelt on at the end of the day. When you hear the click of the belt, think of one thing that "clicked" for you. Or if you have a habit of washing your hands throughout the day or using hand sanitizer, as you clean your hands, think of one thing you appreciate. Pair your email checking habit in the morning with a gratitude email, with no "ask" in it. Just a few moments each morning sending a simple, "Thank you for yesterday when you took over my class so I could use the bathroom; you're a life saver!" or "Thanks for completing that survey I needed; it's appreciated!" can boost your mood and make someone else's day.

Now, let's turn to more ways you can capitalize on your Thrive-o-gram strengths to fold savoring, appreciation, and gratitude in your day.

 **Go-Getter:** Go-Getters love to complete tasks and (if we're being honest with ourselves) receive appreciation. Who doesn't? But if you crush your to-do list and no one notices, give yourself the appreciation you deserve. Stop and savor your achievements each day. Put a smiley face sticker on your to-do list, or as you cross off an item on your list, stop and thank yourself for taking care of it before you move onto the next item.

 **Fascinator:** As someone who loves learning and has a strength in hope, you likely tend toward optimism already. Use that natural positivity to create praise prisms in your classroom and life. If someone thanks you for something, accept it and offer praise back. For example, if a parent thanks you for your extra time after school, thank them for making the time to chat with you as well. If a student thanks you for extra recess time, thank the class for using their time so wisely in the morning to allow for extra recess.

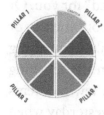 **Creator:** As a future-thinker, you might have a hard time appreciating the present moment. One way to build appreciation and gratitude in your day is to set an alert on your phone or find a gratitude app that pings you at random

intervals in the day. When you hear the ping, stop for a moment and look around for something to appreciate or savor.

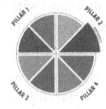

Architect: How can you create a foundation for gratitude? When in your day can you carve out moments of reflection? Think about when you can take brief pauses during the day, perhaps during students' warm-up activities or independent work, to simply sit, breathe, and observe your surroundings. Use these moments to gain perspective, appreciate the safety and comfort of your classroom, and acknowledge the progress and effort of your students.

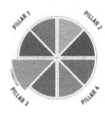

Connector: Teamwork makes the dream work, right? Throughout the day, offer genuine compliments and acknowledgment for students' hard work and cooperation. Use compliment slips or sticky notes as tokens of appreciation, placed on desks, assignments, or backpacks. If you work with older students who may get embarrassed by public praise, email them a short appreciation or give them a note to take home.

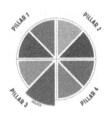

Helper: Kindness is your core strength, so you're going to love embedding more gratitude in your day! One way to do this is to foster gratitude with your students. Have students write a letter to someone who has helped them but whom they've never thanked before. Do the activity with them! This exercise can foster positive emotions and a deeper sense of appreciation.

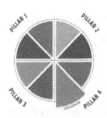

Influencer: Time to take the lead on positivity – you were made for creating gratitude culture at your school! Send appreciation notes to your colleagues, start meetings with sharing a gratitude or appreciation, or create a gratitude wall in your classroom or school.

Nurturer: Your core strength of self-awareness comes in really handy when you are trying to foster a grateful mindset! The next time you catch yourself in negative rumination, try the 2-for-1 technique. For every one negative thought, think of two positive thoughts or positive reframes. For example, if your class is restless and you're getting cranky, you could tell yourself, "My class has a lot of energy that can be harnessed for learning" or "Here's a great opportunity to teach my students self-awareness in a grounding practice."

Your Thriving Road Map

By embedding gratitude practices into the school day, you can create an environment where gratitude is not just a concept but a lived experience, for both you and your students! This approach not only enhances the classroom atmosphere but also teaches students valuable life skills in recognizing and appreciating the good in their lives.

Remember to live in the little moments of gratitude. Get started today! Write down your favorite key takeaway from this chapter that you'd like to start cultivating or reinforcing today!

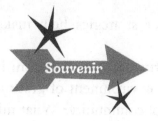

Write down one micro-habit strategy from this chapter that you want to take with you as a souvenir for yourself.

_____

Write down one micro-habit strategy from this chapter that you want to take with you as a souvenir to use at your school or with your students.

_____

Discussion Questions:

1. **Recognizing the Small Moments:** Can you recall a small, seemingly insignificant moment recently that you now realize was a moment of gratitude? How did this moment impact your day?

2. **Implementing Gratitude in the Classroom:** How have you incorporated gratitude into your teaching practices? What activities or routines have you found effective in cultivating a sense of appreciation in your students?

3. **The Daily Gratitude Shift:** What are some of the daily stresses you face, and how can shifting your focus to gratitude change your experience of these stresses? What micro-habit can you cultivate to "Velcro" moments of positivity from the school day in your brain?

4. **Gratitude as a Habit:** Discuss ways you can integrate gratitude more consistently into your daily life. How can habit

stacking or other strategies help make gratitude a regular practice?

5. **Creating a Culture of Appreciation:** How can we, as educators, foster an environment of gratitude and appreciation within our school community? What might be the first step in creating this culture change?

6. **Your Personal Road Map:** Using your Thriving Road Map from Appendix A as a guide, what is one action step you can take immediately to cultivate more work-life alliance? What were your "souvenir" ideas you want to share with students?

Notes

1. Robert Emmons (2010). Why Gratitude Is Good. *Greater Good Magazine*. https://greatergood.berkeley.edu/article/item/why_gratitude_is_good
2. Stacey Kennelly (2012). 10 Steps to Savoring the Good Things in Life. *Greater Good Magazine*. https://greatergood.berkeley.edu/article/item/10_steps_to_savoring_the_good_things_in_life
3. R. A. Emmons and M. E. McCullough (2003). Counting blessings versus burdens: An experimental investigation of gratitude and subjective well-being in daily life. *Journal of Personality and Social Psychology* 84(2), 377–389. https://doi.org/10.1037/0022-3514.84.2.377
4. Jessica Lindsey (2020). Do This in the Afternoon for a Better Workday. *Greater Good Magazine*. https://greatergood.berkeley.edu/article/item/do_this_in_the_afternoon_for_a_better_workday
5. Sabine Sonnentag et al. (2019). Morning Reattachment to Work and Work Engagement During the Day: A Look at Day-Level Mediators. *Sage Journals*. https://journals.sagepub.com/doi/full/10.1177/0149206319829823
6. Shawn Achor (2018). *Big Potential: How Transforming the Pursuit of Success Raises Our Achievement, Happiness, and Well-Being*. New York: Currency.

CHAPTER

10

Thrive Ratio

Before we embark on the crucial last leg on our journey to Thrive Town – understanding and cultivating the "Thrive Ratio" – let's take a moment for reflection.

In Chapter 1, we talked about the psychological state of "flow" where you are using your strengths, doing what you love, and time flies. Think about your current situation. How much of your workday is spent in these flow states? Add up everything in an eight-hour school day as you think about this (I know, I know, we all work more than eight hours most days!).

In an eight-hour day, I spend about _____ (amount of time) in flow, doing what I love.

Now that you have that baseline number, let's talk about why it's so important to think about from a quantitative perspective.

Why the Thrive Ratio Is Essential for Burnout Prevention

The Thrive Ratio is a simple yet powerful concept. Research from the ATP Research Institute and Mayo Clinic suggests that if less than 20% of our work consists of activities we love, the risk of burnout significantly increases. Therefore, ensuring that at least 20% of our day involves engaging in tasks that bring us joy and utilize our strengths can shield us from the negative effects of burnout. Y'all, this equates to only one to two hours in a typical workday. Surely you can work out how to spend just an hour a day doing something fun and meaningful!

Here are some practical ways to implement this concept:

- **Rearview Mirror Reflection:** Start by visualizing your ideal day at work. Imagine the activities, the people around you, what you're wearing, and how you feel. This visualization primes your brain to recognize and seize opportunities to make this ideal day a reality.

- **Small Daily Actions:** Focus on small actions that align with your strengths and bring you joy. This could range from more time doing read alouds with your students, carving out one-on-one time meetings with students to build relationships, creating fun rituals to do with your students, planning a fun lesson, to spending time during your break doing something fun for yourself. Remember, it's about tipping the balance in favor of activities that invigorate you.

- **Being the Thermostat, Not the Thermometer:** This metaphor is about maintaining a consistent, positive energy in the classroom, irrespective of the surrounding chaos. So often our energy moves with the class – when they're low, it brings us down, and when they're dysregulated and high energy, we follow suit and get frazzled ourselves. This is being the thermometer. However, you can be the thermostat instead. By regulating your emotional responses, you provide a stable and reassuring presence for your students, aiding their self-regulation and learning. When your class is at 110 degrees of crazy, you can bring them down with your cool 68 degrees. When your class is at 30 degrees of low energy, you bring them up with your regulated 68 degrees.

- **Cultivating Co-Regulation:** Remember how moods are contagious from Chapter 4? Through sensitive and responsive interactions with students, especially those displaying heightened emotions, you can co-regulate. This process helps students learn to regulate their emotions by mirroring your calm demeanor. One way to remember the importance of co-regulation is remembering one of my favorite quotes by L.R. Knost: "When little people are overwhelmed by big emotions, it's our job to share our calm, not join their chaos." When you have a regulated and vibrant classroom, it positively impacts your Thrive Ratio!

- **Sharing Your Vision:** Once you've envisioned your Thrive Town, share it! Use platforms to share and gain inspiration from fellow educators. To connect with me and our broader Thriving Students community, follow and tag me @thrivingschoolpsych on Instagram or @thrivingstudents on TikTok and use the hashtag #ThriveTown.

- **Embracing the Journey:** Embrace every part of this journey, including the challenges. Learning to enjoy the process and embracing mistakes are as important as the destination!

As we conclude this chapter and our journey together, remember that thriving as an educator isn't just about the big wins or perfect days. It's about consistently integrating small actions, behaviors, and mindsets that uplift you and, by extension, your students. By improving your Thrive Ratio, not only do you combat burnout, but you also foster a more positive and effective learning environment.

Bridging the Research to Your Reality

As we come to the end of this journey, let's pause and soak in a comforting truth: Striving for our own happiness and emotional wellness isn't just a personal perk – it's a professional imperative.

An educator whose emotional climate is steady and positive becomes an effective force in the classroom. You know the vibe. Just think of a day when dark clouds hovered over your mood. Recall the tone of your voice, the types of activities you led, and the accomplishments of the day – or lack thereof. Now think of a day you showed up rested, excited, and happy. You likely found reservoirs of patience and creativity, went that extra mile for your students, and ended the day feeling like you truly made a difference.

This is why self-care is not selfish. Positivity that comes from taking care of your needs not only uplifts you but also illuminates the experiences of everyone around you – most importantly, your students, who are deeply influenced by the emotional atmosphere you cultivate.

Here in Thrive Town, we aim to foster a symbiotic thriving, a communal well-being that benefits both teacher and student, something Angela Watson and I have deemed "co-thriving."

Here are three pivotal understandings to carry with you as you continue to navigate this journey.

Explore the Diversity of Thrive Town

Thrive Town isn't a one-stop destination. It's a constellation of neighborhoods, each unique and ever-changing. As you move through different stages of life, your personal Thrive Town may evolve. Expect multiple destinations and varied paths throughout your career, complete with unexpected detours that may lead you to places you hadn't anticipated. Embrace this fluidity and stay open to the myriad ways you can flourish.

Cherish Where You Are

Enhance your stay in Thrive Town by doing what you love. Take a moment at day's end to reflect: "What sparked joy today? What drained me?" By identifying these elements, you can find ways to weave in more of what elevates your spirit and intersperse it with the less enjoyable tasks. This is about tilting the balance toward joy. Remember the Thrive Ratio research? Just 20% of your day, a mere 90 minutes, spent engaged in activities that bring you flow and fulfillment can drastically amplify your sense of well-being.

Celebrate the Road Traveled

Frequently look back at the path you've trodden. This blend of gratitude and recognition for your achievements nourishes a deep sense of satisfaction. As we reflect on our shared journey, let's reflect the myriad strategies you've explored: from replenishing your positivity to mastering work-life balance, from mindfully selecting your marigold support network to savoring moments of tranquility amidst chaos, from navigating the snarls of bureaucracy to embracing the restorative power of self-compassion, and, finally, journeying along the scenic gratitude route to reignite your passion.

And if you find yourself thinking, "I haven't quite put all this into practice yet," don't fret! Our journey to Thrive Town isn't about planting our flag in the ground once and forever; it's a life-long voyage. We've mapped out the route together, and the next steps on this path belong to you . . .

Micro-Habits to Use Your Thrive-O-Gram Strength

One final habit hack is worth sharing here as we culminate and integrate the various "souvenirs" of mindset and behavioral habit hacks you've picked up and hopefully started to try on for size. Research shows that to change your behavior, you have to make it a part of your identity.

Here's some fun research on how this works. Remember from the introduction that when people say things like "I *vote*" (behavior) they are less likely to vote than people who say "I'm a *voter*" (identity)? So, if you think "I'm not the type of person who can thrive in this environment," it's going to be a heckuva lot harder to change your behaviors to your Thrive Ratio than if you think, "I am the type of person who can bloom where I'm planted."

So, let's turn to more ways you fold your Thrive-o-gram type into your identity as one who thrives by cultivating the Thrive Ratio!

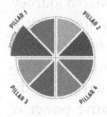 **Go-Getter:** Part of your identity as a Go-Getter is your love for achievement, hope, and living up to your true potential as an educator. Your Thrive Ratio mantra: "I am a Go-Getter. I thrive by crushing my to-do list." So, add some thrive time to your to-do list to increase your Thrive Ratio!

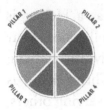

Fascinator: Part of your identity as a Fascinator is your love of learning and hope. Your Thrive Ratio mantra: "I am a Fascinator. I thrive in the deep dive." So, dig into everything you've learned in this book, put your favorite strategies into practice, and keep learning to get to your Thrive Ratio, Fascinator!

Creator: Part of your identity as a Creator is your creativity and courage. Your Thrive Ratio mantra: "I thrive when I am creating solutions." So get creating! What is the solution to moving toward a better Thrive Ratio? Pick your favorite strategies from this book and create a custom plan for yourself!

Architect: Part of your identity as an Architect is your perspective and courage. Your Thrive Ratio mantra: "I thrive by creating a plan." So get planning, my Architect friend! Write out your own road map to get to your Thrive Ratio with all the things that resonated with you from the book!

Connector: Part of your identity as a Connector is your teamwork and social intelligence. Your Thrive Ratio mantra: "I thrive when I am connecting people and ideas." Can you connect the thriving dots for yourself and those around you? Think back on the strategies that resonate with you, practice them yourself, and share with your students and colleagues to get a coalition of thrivers!

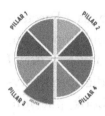

Helper: Part of your identity as a Helper is your kindness and social intelligence. Your Thrive Ratio mantra: "I thrive by helping others." As a Helper, your Thrive Ratio is likely enhanced when you are serving others, but don't forget about self-kindness, too! Your well-being is the catalyst for helping your Thrive Ratio and having emotional energy to give to others.

Influencer: Part of your identity as an Influencer is your leadership and self-compassion. Your Thrive Ratio mantra: "I thrive when I change minds." Part of your identity as an Influencer can include being the type of person who leads by example. When you improve your Thrive Ratio, you serve as a model for others around you to do the same!

Nurturer: Part of your identity as a Nurturer is your self-compassion and self-awareness. Your Thrive Ratio mantra: "I thrive when I nurture my needs." So, how can you build in time to nurture your needs in your day to enhance your Thrive Ratio? Take a few ideas from the book that resonated with you and fold them into your daily routine!

Your Thriving Road Map

Yay, we made it . . . or did we?!? As we metaphorically roll into the vibrant streets of Thrive Town, let's pause for a moment. Have we really arrived, or is this just another scenic spot on a much longer journey? The truth, as we've discovered together, is that thriving as an educator isn't about reaching a final destination. Just like our students are never "done" learning, we are never "done" learning about how to thrive!

Throughout this book, we've equipped ourselves with keys to success, ready to tackle any roadblocks that the path to thriving as an educator might throw at us. What have been the highlights of this trip for you? The snacks? The coffee? Getting off the struggle bus and hopping on the thriving party bus?

For me, it's been realizing the importance of co-thriving – the idea that when we, as educators, are thriving, our students naturally follow suit. We become "living lesson plans," embodying the very principles we teach.

If you've found yourself taking unexpected detours toward Burnout Town, remember, you're not alone. There's comfort and strength in our collective experience and understanding that becoming the educator you aspire to be is more about letting go of the baggage that you don't need on your journey than lugging it around thinking it's the only way to travel.

What I'm advocating here is a form of radical acceptance – embracing who you are in your teaching and education journey and finding peace in that authenticity. It's about showing up as the best version of yourself, not by overexerting, but by harmoniously co-thriving with your students.

If there's one thing to take away from our time together, let it be this: *Enjoy the ride, bumps and all.* This includes embracing the challenges, the uncertainties, and the joyful moments alike. Remember, every bump, every twist and turn, is part of what shapes you as an educator.

As we conclude this part of our journey, I want to express my gratitude for your companionship on this ride. Your commitment to personal growth and student thriving is what makes this journey so worthwhile. Let's grab one more souvenir!

Remember, when you thrive, your students thrive!

Discussion Questions:

1. **Finding Flow:** Reflect on your workday and share a specific activity that consistently puts you in a state of flow. How can you leverage this insight to increase the time you spend in these fulfilling activities?

2. **Building the Thrive Ratio:** Discuss ways you might increase your Thrive Ratio. What activities or tasks could you delegate or minimize to spend more time in your flow state?

3. **The Emotional Climate of Your Classroom:** How do you maintain a positive and consistent emotional climate in your classroom? Share strategies for being the "thermostat" rather than the "thermometer."

4. **Co-Regulation in Practice:** Can you share a time when you successfully practiced co-regulation in your classroom? How did it impact the students' behavior and the overall classroom environment?

5. **Sharing the Vision of Thrive Town:** How can we, as a community of educators, support each other in creating and maintaining our own versions of Thrive Town? What collaborative practices might we develop to foster co-thriving in our schools?

6. **Your Personal Road Map:** Using your Thriving Road Map from Appendix A as a guide, what is one action step you can take immediately to cultivate your Thrive Ratio? What are your "souvenir" ideas you want to share with students?

Appendix A

Small Habits Create Big Changes

Your Personalized Thriving Road Map

with Dr. Rebecca Branstetter

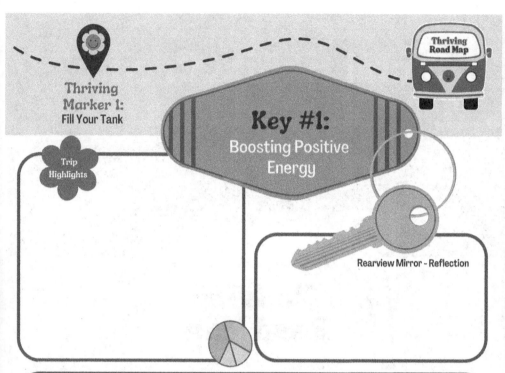

Thriving Marker 1:
Fill Your Tank

Trip Highlights

Key #1:
Boosting Positive Energy

Rearview Mirror - Reflection

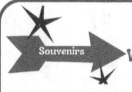

Souvenirs   What is one take-home souvenir for myself?

What is one souvenir to share with my school/students?

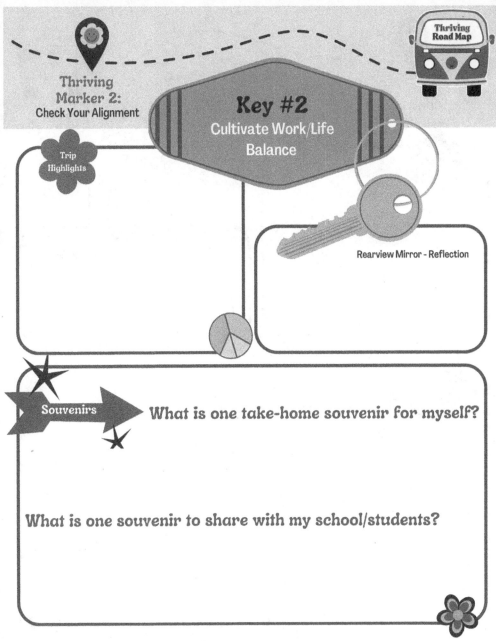

Thriving
Marker 2:
Check Your Alignment

Key #2
Cultivate Work/Life
Balance

Trip
Highlights

Rearview Mirror - Reflection

Souvenirs   What is one take-home souvenir for myself?

What is one souvenir to share with my school/students?

© Thriving Students Collective

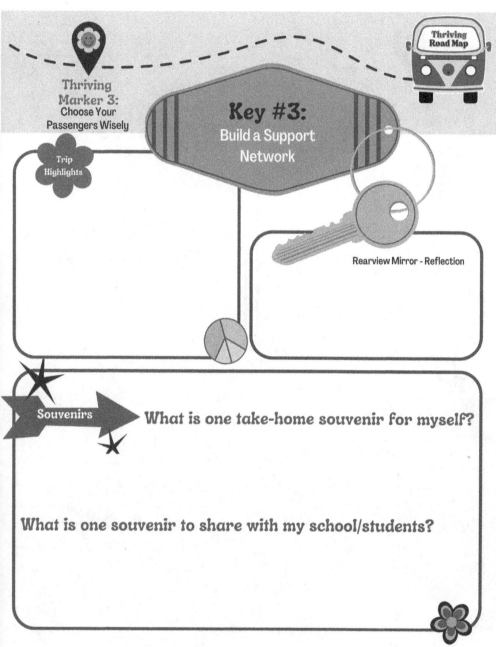

Thriving Road Map

Thriving Marker 3:
Choose Your Passengers Wisely

Key #3:
Build a Support Network

Trip Highlights

Rearview Mirror - Reflection

Souvenirs

What is one take-home souvenir for myself?

What is one souvenir to share with my school/students?

© Thriving Students Collective

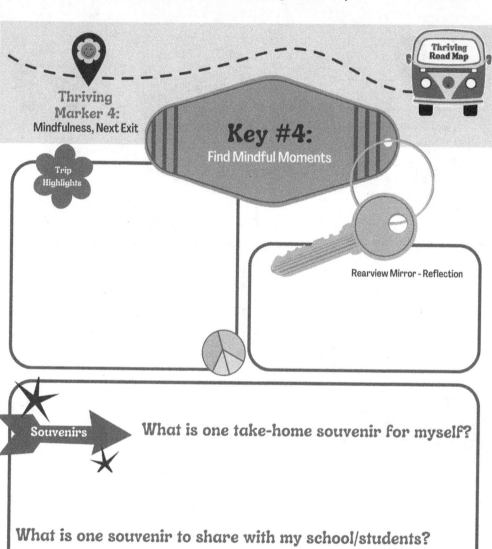

Thriving
Marker 4:
Mindfulness, Next Exit

Key #4:
Find Mindful Moments

Trip
Highlights

Rearview Mirror - Reflection

Souvenirs → What is one take-home souvenir for myself?

What is one souvenir to share with my school/students?

© Thriving Students Collective

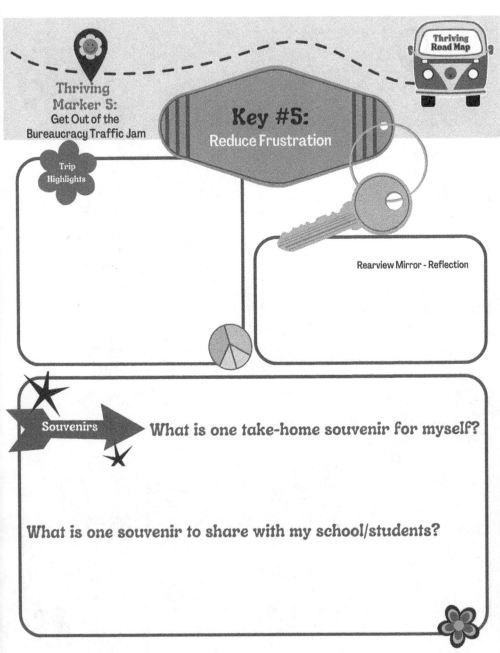

Thriving
Marker 5:
Get Out of the
Bureaucracy Traffic Jam

Key #5:
Reduce Frustration

Trip Highlights

Rearview Mirror - Reflection

Souvenirs

What is one take-home souvenir for myself?

What is one souvenir to share with my school/students?

© Thriving Students Collective

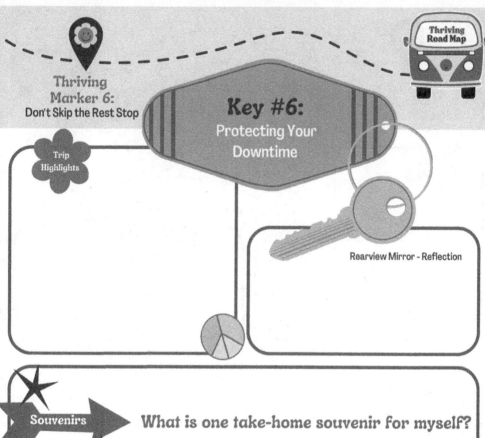

Thriving
Marker 6:
Don't Skip the Rest Stop

Key #6:
Protecting Your
Downtime

Trip
Highlights

Rearview Mirror - Reflection

Souvenirs   **What is one take-home souvenir for myself?**

What is one souvenir to share with my school/students?

© Thriving Students Collective

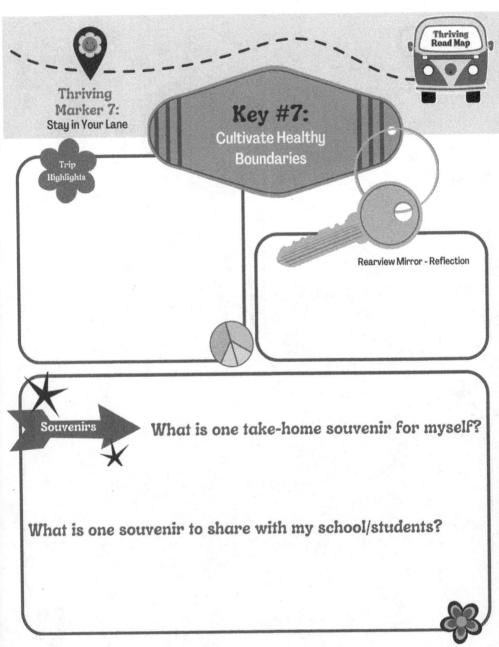

Thriving
Road Map

**Thriving
Marker 7:**
Stay in Your Lane

Key #7:
Cultivate Healthy
Boundaries

Trip
Highlights

Rearview Mirror - Reflection

Souvenirs   **What is one take-home souvenir for myself?**

What is one souvenir to share with my school/students?

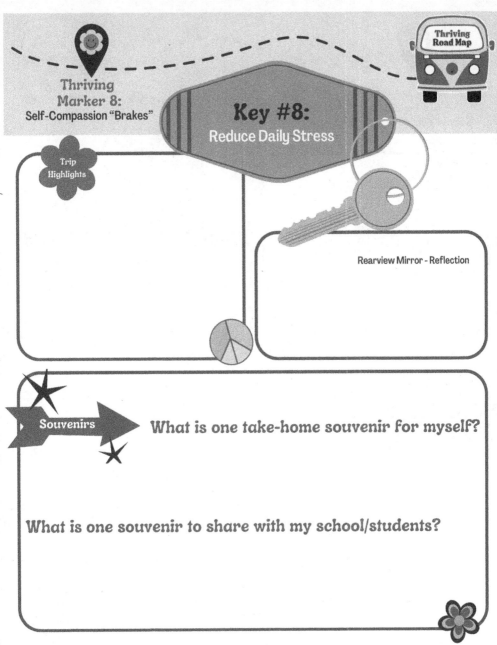

Thriving
Marker 8:
Self-Compassion "Brakes"

Key #8:
Reduce Daily Stress

Trip
Highlights

Rearview Mirror - Reflection

Souvenirs

What is one take-home souvenir for myself?

What is one souvenir to share with my school/students?

© Thriving Students Collective

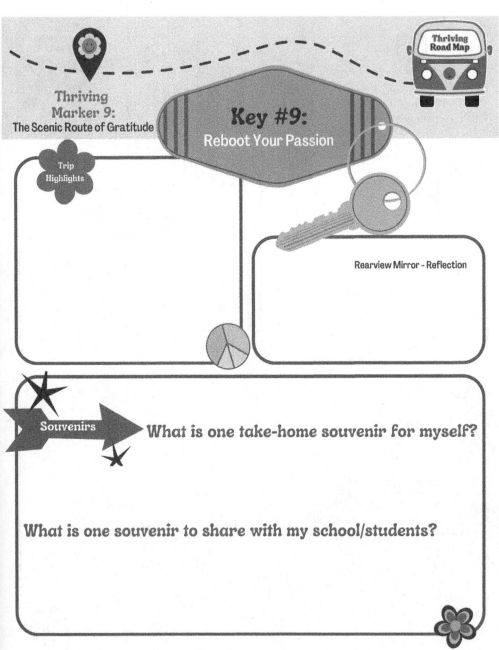

Thriving
Marker 9:
The Scenic Route of Gratitude

Key #9:
Reboot Your Passion

Trip
Highlights

Rearview Mirror - Reflection

Souvenirs   What is one take-home souvenir for myself?

What is one souvenir to share with my school/students?

© Thriving Students Collective

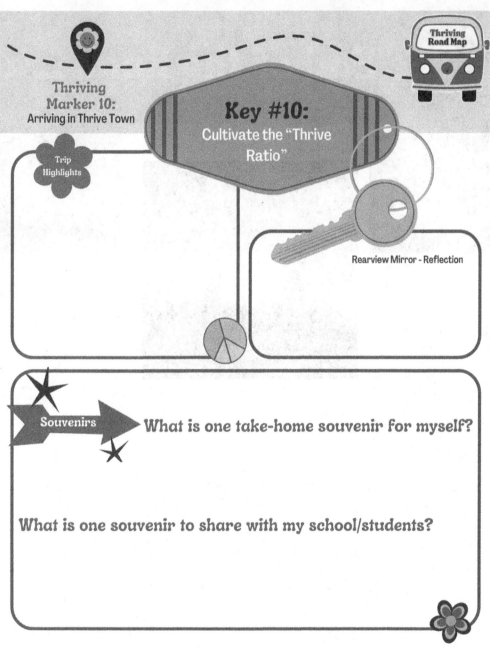

Thriving
Marker 10:
Arriving in Thrive Town

Key #10:
Cultivate the "Thrive Ratio"

Trip Highlights

Rearview Mirror - Reflection

Souvenirs   What is one take-home souvenir for myself?

What is one souvenir to share with my school/students?

© Thriving Students Collective

The End of the Road...

OR IS IT?

100k views

View all 1205 comments

1 DAYS AGO

Stay in Touch with Dr. Branstetter!

Instagram: @thrivingschoolpsych
TikTok: @thrivingstudents
www.thrivingstudents.com

Appendix B:
Journey to Thrive Town: A Guide for School and District Leaders

H ello there! Chances are, if you're reading this, you're a leader who has decided that staff wellness initiatives need to move beyond encouraging educators to simply "do more self-care" after work. You're likely looking for research-backed strategies that staff can do not just after work, but at work, where the stress is actually happening. With teachers showing the highest burnout rate of any profession in the United States, and student mental health and learning needs at an all-time high, we are in a two-fold crisis: *Students' needs are up, and everyone's bandwidth is down.*

As a leader, you are likely feeling this stress acutely, on a daily basis. Maybe you're one of the many school leaders I've spoken with who tell me they stay awake at night wondering how to break the cycle of "hiring in the front door and having folks leave out the back door." Or maybe your students have escalating behavioral and mental health needs and you don't have enough school psychologists or mental health providers to support the growing need. And perhaps it feels like every time you open your inbox, answer the phone, or hear a knock on your door, it's another crisis, unhappy parent, or discouraged teacher asking for your support.

As you look to innovate, you might be looking for new ways to create a culture shift in your school, where educators on the brink of burnout can reclaim their joy. You might be seeking new ways to support your staff, shifting the collective mindset that self-care is a "nice to have" thing you do after work to a "need to have" that is actually doable in the school day. And as an educator in a leadership position, you are probably pretty interested in the strategies for yourself!

The good news is that the strategies in this book will be a tool for you to lead by example – a chance to "walk the walk" and foster a climate where you set the positive emotional tone for your team. By doing so, you will be building a culture of connection and collective efficacy that educators *can* thrive in challenging circumstances. You'll also have science-backed ways to show that tending to the well-being of the adults in your building is actually one of the best interventions for your students.

Whether you're hosting a teacher book club or taking your full staff on the full journey with the companion online masterclass, *How to Reverse Educator Burnout*, this book will help you plan out your journey to "Thrive Town" – a place where educators co-thrive with their students.

Are you interested in learning more about the companion online masterclass, How to Reverse Educator Burnout? Visit www.thrivingstudents.com/reverseburnout *or scan this QR code.*

As you'll learn throughout this book, you're about to embark on a journey! The book is built on the metaphor of a road trip to Thrive Town, where you'll help your team get to a destination where they are engaged, empowered, and excited about showing up to school. Boosting morale and reducing burnout is a worthy goal in and of itself, but part of your journey is also cultivating the ripple effect where a culture shift in turn also boosts the academic and social-emotional growth of students.

Along the way, you and your team will learn how to navigate inevitable bumps and detours in the road. You may have staff that are skeptical that Thrive Town even exists and are not quite ready to hop on the bus with you. That's okay! When you start with understanding and practicing the principles yourself, you will have more patience for the inevitable chatter in the backseats of "Are we there yet?", "I'm tiiiiiiired," and "But I don't like this way!" vibes along the way. Like all initiatives, start with a coalition of the willing, get a critical mass on the bus, and they will become ambassadors and cheerleaders along the way.

As you embark on this critical journey with your team, think of yourselves as seasoned travelers who have a clear vision of the destination. Your role is not just to lead the way but to ensure that everyone arrives together, refreshed and ready to engage anew. Here are a few tips from leaders who have traveled this road before!

Preparing for the Trip

Step 1: Choose Your Own Adventure!

This book is a companion to our *How to Reverse Educator Burnout* masterclass. While you do not need to have the online course to

facilitate your team through the book, you can visit www.
thrivingstudents.com/reverseburnout to consider a deeper dive
as you go through the book, or as an added feature after you've
read the book.

How are the book and course different and complementary?
This book covers the research on burnout and provides the "too
small to fail" micro-habit strategies to get started on your journey to Thrive Town. After reading each chapter, you will have a
great jumping off point for further discussion with the end-of-
chapter questions.

The online course offers a deeper dive into the practical side
of the equation – how these burnout prevention concepts and
micro-habits are specifically integrated into daily routines and in
the classroom. The course has bonus content with expert teachers in productivity, co-regulation, and classroom management
(since behaviors are a big source of stress!) that bring the ideas
further to life. The course also provides bonus videos on how to
fold in burnout prevention into existing diversity, equity, and
inclusion initiatives.

The videos in the masterclass also serve as "scenic views"
along your route, providing visual and auditory reinforcement
of the concepts your team is reading about. They offer both a
break from the written word and an alternative method to
engage with the material, catering to diverse learning styles
within your team.

If you've opted to purchase licenses for the companion course
for your team, schedule a viewing at a cadence that makes sense
for you! Many leaders opt for playing a short video at the top of
a staff meeting or at a scheduled professional development, and
then have a discussion in a professional learning community.
Other leaders prefer to provide their staff with the course to give
them the freedom to go at their own pace. You know your staff
best and what will work for them!

Step 2: Read the Chapter

Start each session of your journey by reading the designated chapter yourself. This initial reading is your road map; it outlines the terrain you'll cover together and the landmarks of knowledge and strategies designed to combat educator burnout. Your understanding and insights will set the tone for the journey ahead and prepare you to guide your team effectively. Consider filling out the "Thriving Road Map" provided at the end of this book yourself so you will be able to better facilitate your team in completing theirs.

You can also add notes on what you want to emphasize with your staff, or provide supplemental resources on the theme. For instance, after reading the chapter on mindfulness, you might want to collaborate with a leader on your team to create a handout with all the mindfulness resources your school offers staff and students to share when you discuss the chapter.

Step 3: Facilitate a Discussion

After reading the chapter, gather your team for a discussion. For instance, you might have a "Lunch and Learn" opportunity where staff can gather to enjoy food, each other's company, and discuss the chapter. Or, you can dedicate 10-15 minutes of your staff meeting, professional learning community time, or team meetings to discuss the chapter in small groups or as a whole group.

The purpose of the gathering is to check understanding, share insights, and personalize the information to the specific educational environment. It's the part of the trip where everyone gets to speak about what they've seen and heard, what resonates with them, and what they find challenging.

Step 4: Make it Visible

To keep the ideas from the chapters at the forefront of your staff's minds, consider making a visual reminder in your school. Perhaps in your staff room, create a bulletin board on the concept you are discussing. To empower your staff and create buy in, after the discussion of the chapter, ask if anyone wants to take the lead on creating a shared vision of the concept. Chances are, you have some crafty and creative folks who would find it to be fun! They may even want to engage student leaders in the project, as part of the goal of the book is to learn the ideas ourselves, and then teach our students the concepts, too! (And please, if you make something cool with your staff, take a picture and share on social media with the hashtag #thrivetown and tag me @thrivingschoolpsych so the larger community can be inspired!)

Engaging Your Team in Thrive Town

Create a Safe Environment

As the leader, your first task is to create a safe and open environment where your staff feels comfortable sharing their experiences and feelings. Co-create group norms for discussions such as "Listen to learn, not to fix" or "Take space and leave space" – where people balance sharing (take space) but also actively listening to their colleagues (leave space).

Use Discussion Prompts

At the end of each chapter, utilize the discussion prompts provided. These are designed to encourage deep reflection and meaningful conversations. Each question should guide your team to consider how the strategies discussed can be implemented or adapted to your specific context.

Encourage Personal Reflection

In addition to group discussions, encourage your educators to reflect personally on each chapter. Personal reflection allows individuals to internalize what they've learned and to think about practical applications of their new knowledge. At the end of the book, there is a downloadable/printable Thriving Road Map where your team can process, reflect, and ideate on the content privately before they share out with the larger group.

Action Planning

As a final step in your Thrive Town visit, help your team develop an action plan. What specific steps will they take to apply what they've learned? How will they support each other in this journey? This plan should be a living document, revisited and revised as you continue your travels through each chapter of the book.

Conclusion

Leading your team through *Small Habits create Big Change* or *How to Reverse Teacher Burnout course* is akin to guiding them on a journey to a place where the air is clearer, the scenery is inspiring, and the path leads to rejuvenation. As a district leader, your role is to map the route, support your travelers, and ensure that everyone reaches Thrive Town together, equipped with new tools and a renewed spirit to continue their important work in education.

By taking these steps – reading together, potentially watching the companion materials, and engaging in deep, thoughtful discussions – you are not only addressing the issue of burnout but are also fostering a culture of continuous improvement and support. Here's to a successful journey toward Thrive Town! Hop in . . .

Epilogue

Ironically, I ignored my research-based awesome advice last weekend. I was up on a few deadlines (including this book!) and decided to spend all weekend getting "caught up." I plowed through my inbox, did hours of research for my bibliography, and muscled my way through creating slides for a new training I was doing for a school district on executive functioning. While I did feel productive and accomplished (I'm a Thrive-o-gram Go-Getter!), I also felt a little resentful and tired. My beautiful inbox zero I had worked so hard on was full again on Monday, but I was too tired to even look at it. And then I shamed myself for not knowing better. I mean, I literally have a whole company dedicated to ending burnout and I am writing a book that told people not to do this! (And then, I shamed myself for shaming myself . . . sigh.) I suppose I'm living proof that we are all perpetually works in progress!

As an educator, you are likely familiar with the idea of the "spiraling curriculum" for your students. You introduce a concept, and then revisit it, deepen it, and build on it. I'm here to tell you that learning to beat burnout and staying on the path to Thrive Town is also a spiraling curriculum process!

Change is not a one-time event, y'all!

If you are human, you are likely to start out strong with new ideas from this book. The dopamine hit of new ideas and future-you potential will jump start your Thrive Town bus engine. You'll commit to taking action, practice your new micro-habits, and start to see changes – hurray! More dopamine!

And then, probably, you'll encounter a roadblock on your happy journey to Thrive Town, and because (as the saying goes) we are creatures of habit, you revert back to your old habit factory settings. Like me, maybe you enter a particularly stressful time period, and while caught up in fight/flight/freeze stress, you default to an old way of being (like in my moment of multiple deadline stress, I defaulted to my old habit of overworking without rest).

I share this not to bum you out, but to normalize that there *will* be setbacks, so when you encounter them, you don't give up and say, "Welp, looks like I'll never get to Thrive Town!" Remember the spiraling curriculum: you learn the neuroscience that rested and happy minds are more productive, you try it out and it works, you get overwhelmed and forget what you learned, and then you reboot the habit (maybe with a marigold buddy) and so the grooves of the new habit start to be deeper than the old grooves. And you forgive yourself for backslides and you say what you would to a good friend: It's okay my friend. Change takes time!

If I have one last piece of advice, it's to *be gentle with yourself* as you embrace this spiraling curriculum of personal growth, professional well-being, and co-thriving with your students. On any journey, there can be unexpected "plot twists" of stormy weather, travel delays, and interesting detours, and your journey to Thrive Town is no different!

And now, I'm off to rest . . . thank you for being with me on this brave and bold adventure!

Take care,
Rebecca

Index

Page numbers followed by *f* refer to figures.